**THE OFFICIAL**
**TOUR DE FRANCE**

# ROAD CYCLING
# TRAINING GUIDE

This edition published in 2020
by Welbeck Non-Fiction Limited
20 Mortimer Street, London W1T 3JW

Copyright © Welbeck Publishing Group
2020
Tour de France trademark copyright ©
ASO/STF 2020

A CIP catalogue record for this book is
available from the British Library

ISBN 978-1-78739-460-5

Editorial Director: Martin Corteel
Design Manager: Luke Griffin
Design: RockJaw Creative
Picture Research: Paul Langan
Production: Rachel Burgess

Printed in Spain

**Author's Acknowledgements**

Thank you to everyone at Welbeck Publishing for guiding me
through this first authoring experience, especially Martin who has
been a calming figure during hectic times.

Thank you to every rider, coach, team member and press officer who
I have hassled for quotes and have helped create this book — none
more so than Nico Portal who will be truly missed by the entire
cycling fraternity.

To my wife Laura, thank you for not only giving me love and
support every day, but also pitching up eight hours before the
peloton arrived on the Champs-Élysées ahead of the 2012 Tour de
France final stage — that is true love.

To Mum, Dad and Charlotte, thank you for continuously believing
in whatever I put my mind to. As well as starting my cycling journey
by pushing me in a buggy to watch the Tour peloton zoom down
Ditchling Road in Brighton in 1994.

Lastly to my riding partner Will, who I hope will take all the advice
in this book to beat me up Alpe d'Huez one day…

THE OFFICIAL
TOUR DE FRANCE

# ROAD CYCLING
# TRAINING GUIDE

Everything you need to know
to ride like the professionals

Paul Knott

W

WELBECK

# CONTENTS

**The Tour de France is arguably the toughest sporting event in the world. Three weeks of bike racing, over 21 stages, tackling gruelling climbs, daring descents and nail-biting sprint finishes are just some of the challenges riders face on the open roads.**

For amateurs the dream of tackling just one of these stages has become a reality with *Gran Fondos* and *sportives* tackling many of the famous climbs and roads featured in the Grand Tours, with the *Étape du Tour* arguably the most iconic of all. With an ever-changing route each year cresting some of the legendary climbs that grace the Tour de France, it is the biggest challenge most amateur riders will face in their lives.

For mere mortals to take on this challenge they must prepare both physically and psychologically for the almost overwhelming task ahead. This can begin by setting goals for the season, ensuring a quality bike fit has taken place and knowing the types of training sessions necessary to see them reach their potential come the big day.

In modern-day cycling there are also so many tools amateur cyclists can embrace to enhance their performance. These include: the rise of data as a training tool; the knowledge of nutritional needs required to fuel multiple-hour bike rides; and honing bike-handling skills that will guide a cyclist across terrain which are regularly encountered by professional tour cyclists.

This is the journey many pro riders will undertake every season on their way to racing *Le Grand Boucle*. We have

▶ The Champs-Elysées is arguably the finest setting for a sporting event finale in the world.

spoken to former Tour de France stage and overall winners as well as trainers, coaches, nutritionists and chefs from inside the UCI WorldTour teams. They offer amateur cyclists the best advice on how to train for and feel ready for an epic day out on the bike. This may well be a big day out taming some of the mountainous beasts that sit in the Pyrenees, Alps and Vosges ranges that are a mainstay of Tour de France history themselves.

If you want some insight into how the pros train, how to improve your nutrition, training advice in preparation for your biggest challenge on the bike at the *Étape du Tour*, or other personal goals, the official *Tour de France Road Cycling Training Guide Book* will help you achieve them.

▼ Conquering the climbs is as much of a challenge for amateurs as it is for the professionals.

Riding overseas in the vast mountain ranges can give cyclists some of the most satisfying riding experiences.

Plotting out your season and specific training plans is key to achieving your goals for the year ahead.

CHAPTER 1

# PLANNING YOUR TRAINING

Improving your cycling performance isn't achieved on pure luck alone. Having a goal at the end of a structured training programme, which is both achievable and adaptable, is the best way to succeed. Being able to modify it for mini goals, fitness test successes, as well as illness and injuries along the way, will all be crucial factors in making your plan work for you.

# GOAL SETTING

▲ Utilising the advice and knowledge of a coach can be really useful to setting achievable and realistic goals.

▶ Once your goals are set in writing, it will give you a real motivational to get out on the road and reach it.

**Designing a training programme can seem a daunting task, but it need not be if you are realistic with your time available, and set sensible training and event goals at the end of it. Combining both of these aspects, and being pragmatic with what is achievable, is key to executing your ultimate plan throughout the year.**

It doesn't matter if your goal is months, weeks or days away. Setting mini targets and writing a plan down on paper makes it a lot easier to keep on top of your schedule. Being unrealistic about work or personal commitments or the goal itself means you are far more likely to fall behind a proposed plan or miss your target altogether.

Ultimately, though you should always keep focused on your goal, whether this is to complete a *Grand Fondo*, or achieve a certain time, ensuring that you aren't jeopardising your riding and subsequently your goal with poor training, nutrition or recovery choices should be adhered to.

One way of ensuring your goals are achievable is to use the SMART acronym. This highlights that your goals are **S**pecific, **M**easurable, **A**greed, **R**ealistic and **T**ime-appropriate. Applying each measure to the goals you have planned will give you an answer as to whether it is a goal worth setting or if it needs tweaking.

**Specific:** Is your goal to complete a ride, aim for a certain time or reach a certain standard?

**Measurable:** Setting markers throughout to the year to ensure you are on track can be key, whether it is to ride 60 kilometres non-stop by April or raise your FTP to a certain level before a target ride in midseason.

**Agreed:** Having an agreed goal with a coach, friend or family member can make sure that your and another person believe it is attainable.

**Realistic:** With hard work and planning most goals are realistic, but it is a case of deciding that for yourself and perhaps, most importantly, if they can be achieved within the challenges of your day-to-day life.

**Time-appropriate:** It is inevitable, from time to time, that we will have to juggle our work, life and training. Making sure your goal takes all these factors into account is key to whether you will be able to achieve it.

- Be sure to mix up your workouts between different disciplines. Incorporating road, track, mountain bike and turbo sessions into your training plan not only breaks up the tedium of repetitive rides but also improves individual bike-handling skills.
- Adjust your training plan if you feel you aren't getting the most out of it. This should be seen as the map to your ultimate goal and if you feel that it isn't working, then don't be afraid to change it.
- Don't feel that you can't ride with others during your training plan. Incorporating group rides into your schedule are crucial to achieving your goals and also making it enjoyable at the same time.
- Be realistic about the amount of time you have available to train as building in time for recovery, work and family commitments are important. Don't become obsessive and let training take over your life.
- Listen to your body and make sure you don't force yourself through injuries to keep up with your programme. Ultimately, this could lead to greater time off the bike and mean you will lose out in the long run.
- Allow for flexibility within your training plan for inclement weather or any unexpected events that may crop up. If poor weather falls on a day where a long ride is scheduled then tweaking the week's schedule should be more than feasible.

▼ Reassessing your goals throughout the year is key to staying on track throughout the season.

# YEARLY PLANNING

▲ Setting out your goals for the year can keep your motivation high throughout the season.

**It can often be tricky to remain motivated, inspired and have the drive to work towards an event a number of months down the line. This is especially so if you are dividing 365 days into an achievable and workable plan across a whole year. It is key to remember that with yearly planning, there is no such thing as "one plan fits all".**

However, one way of structuring your training into a more manageable way is to set up different length cycles through periodization: one based around the long-term goal for the season; another for a medium-term plan; and a third for the short-term target. Applying these cycles will not only help structure rest periods in the plan to help facilitate recovery but also will help encourage the training effect on your cardio-vascular system and muscles. This will ultimately increase your performance on the bike.

It is important to remember, however, that these cycles are not the be-all and end-all, but are helpful in following a structured programme. This can be planned from the beginning your training period and these cycles can be used across training in other sports, each with their own traits.

A macro-cycle is the longest of the three cycles, and incorporates a year-long – 52-week – plan including all the endurance rides, intensity efforts, the big event ride itself and the recovery period required afterwards. The best way to plan your macro-cycle is to mark out your training plan when your key event is and work back to certain dates by when you want to achieve your targets. Because of the length of this training cycle it is important to remember – like all training plans – it is more than likely it will change from time to time, whether it is implementing goals, training focuses throughout the year or ensuring that you implement drop-down weeks and tapering before the actual event day.

A meso-cycle is the most adaptable training cycle of the three, varying between three and four weeks in length, and designed to accomplish a particular goal. This may be building towards a warm-up event or distance while preparing an overall goal, or perhaps just a focus over a sustained period of specific training. There are other ways meso-cycles can be implemented, through block training – which may consist of 16 days of hard training followed by five days of recovery. Although this can be effective for some, it is usually advisable to apply this under the tutelage of a cycling coach.

A micro-cycle is the shortest training block, typically lasting about a week, and focusing on a specific goal or type of training to achieve a certain aspect of the training effect. This is similar to a meso-cycle's goal, but on a shorter and much more focused level. This could be themed around a number of endurance rides within a week to increase aerobic capacity; paying greater attention to off-the-bike training, with a focus on strength and core training; or even just a drop-down week to focus on rest and recovery.

# WHAT ONE PIECE OF ADVICE WOULD YOU PASS ON TO AMATEURS?

**MITCHELL DOCKER – EF PRO CYCLING**

"Consistency is key. A lot of people go hard and then they do nothing. They are motivated to train over the summer and then the winter rolls around and they can't be bothered any more. When it is good weather, just do what you need to do because you've got to save up those psychological matches for those hard days and still want it. By keeping that consistency, you don't have to do a seven-hour day and then have four days off; you can do a few rides over a few days and avoid that big blowout."

◄ After years of training, Docker understands what works best for him to reach his peak fitness at the right time.

# STRUCTURING YOUR TRAINING WEEK

▲ Riding with club mates or friends is a great way to ensure you all keep on track for your goals.

**As much as we'd like to complete every part of our training session and follow every single part of our training week, down to individual seconds in each session, it is not always possible to make sure that this happens. This may be down to family life, work or sometimes Mother Nature having her say on matters.**

Therefore, ensuring that your training week is adaptable and flexible to accommodate last minute challenges or hurdles is just as crucial as making sure the sessions themselves are correct for the type of riding goals you want to achieve. Some of these factors and challenges are common amongst most cyclists and must be thought of when plotting out your training week.

- **Work life balance:** As much as we would love to live the lives of a professional cyclist, with unlimited time to train, rest and recover, the majority of us will have to juggle work, family and a social life alongside our training week. Therefore ensuring your sessions and training week are plotted in a way that can handle your life outside of cycling, without causing unnecessary stress, will not only be beneficial to ensure you actually complete each session, but also mean you don't become overwhelmed psychologically as well. One way of combating this is to utilise your commute as part of your training session. If your place of work has bike storage and changing facilities then it can start and finish your working day on the right step.

## HOW TO KEEP YOUR WEEKLY MOTIVATION HIGH

There will be some weeks when you may not feel physically ready for a stint of hard training, but there are a number of ways to keep your morale high. This may be from combining sessions with friends or club-mates, or joining cycling specific social media training groups that can give encouragement and advice. Even the simple act of putting training plan notes, highlighting the good rides you have already completed, or your goal around your house can help keep your motivation high and push you on to achieve it.

- **Don't risk it with the weather:** The adage, "there is no such thing as bad weather, only unsuitable clothing" applies to cycling as much as to any other sport. However, there may be times, based on the weather that day, when it is wiser to switch sessions for not only your enjoyment but also physical benefit and safety out on the road. Whether the reasons are because of icy roads, freezing fog or being forced to squeeze a climbing session in the sweltering midday summer sun, being able to adapt the timings or day of certain sessions can be beneficial in the short term and the long run.

- **Injuries and illness can happen to anyone:** It may be frustrating to pick up injuries or illnesses, but unfortunately they are inevitable for most cyclists, especially those who push their bodies to the limit. Recognising these signs of injury and illness – and taking the specific recovery time off the bike – is key, no matter what your training plan says. Trying to push your body to ride at a certain effort it can't match, adding in an extra training day that wasn't part of the original plan – or forcing yourself to get back into a training plan too early – may be more harmful to you in the long term than beneficial in the short run.

▼ If you can switch your week around to avoid bad weather then make sure you adapt your schedule accordingly.

# FITNESS TESTING

▲ Testing can give fascinating results which can help improve your training structure.

**Designing a structured training plan, or following one a coach has laid out for you, is key to achieving your end target result. But at the beginning of the season – or during the season itself – it can be useful to test your fitness to ensure your training zone levels are correct for your physiological potential.**

There are a number of testing methods to discover your fitness levels, with many measures available for different types of training aspect. Two major tests which amateurs and professionals both use to find definitive training zone numbers are the VO2 max test and an FTP test.

The VO2 max test is based around the maximum rate of oxygen uptake, which is determined by the cardiovascular system's ability to deliver blood – and oxygen – to the muscles and their subsequent ability to use it. VO2 max is typically measured

in relation to body weight to give us a relative number that can be compared across riders of all shapes and sizes. The result can give a strong indication on the maximum aerobic potential of a cyclist and it is an important physiological marker of their cycling performance. However, the VO2 max test can only accurately be conducted in laboratory conditions where a cyclist's exhaled and inhaled air can be collected in giant air bags and then analysed by gas analysis system.

Whilst laboratory settings can give the most accurate measure of fitness

## FTP TEST

Multiply your testing effort average power result by 0.95 to find your FTP.

| Test time | Effort |
|-----------|--------|
| 0–10 | Gentle warm up spin |
| 10–25 | Three sets of one-minute fast cadence, one-minute easy, three-minute spin |
| 25–30 | Five-minute all out effort |
| 30–40 | 10-minute recovery spin |
| 40–60 | 20-minute all out testing effort |
| 60–70 | Cool down period |

▶ The pro's will typically have a lot of their pre-season testing at the beginning of the season to see what shape they are in.

results, most riders won't have access to these facilities. This makes the FTP (functional threshold power) test a far easier way to measure fitness over time and can be used to adjust training power zones. The number of your FTP is effectively the average power output you can sustain for one hour. There are many ways to complete an FTP test, with many stationary bikes and online training programmes having them built into their systems to carry out. But rather than completing an hour-long effort – which can have accuracy issues amongst other problems – an hour-long session with a 20-minute test set within it can give more accurate end results:

◄ Fitness testing can be and ultimately should be gruelling to find out your peak performance levels.

## HOW THE PROS ARE TESTED:

**KOEN PELGRIM – DECEUNINCK-QUICK STEP COACH**
"We do a number of different tests throughout the season for different reasons. Before the season, everybody has medical testing which is more to see if they are healthy, and it includes a cardiac check to make sure they are allowed and ready to race. But, from a performance perspective, we do separate tests in December and January and then during the season – if we can't get enough information out of our racing or training data – at our testing facility in Belgium.

But before the camp we test all the Belgian riders in Belgium for body composition, body-fat percentage and muscle mass. We also do a sprint test and determine thresholds based on lactate testing and aerobic capacity. At this point, we have the whole picture ready when they start the camp and we can evaluate them again in January to see how it has evolved.

If you compare early December readings with those at the end of January, it can make quite a big difference, because in early December they have just started training and haven't been completing big rides. From then on we do two camps in that period and a lot of things can and should change. We can still change training slightly before they start racing, so it's always a good period to see how they've been responding to the training.

To conquer all terrains you have to adapt your training accordingly.

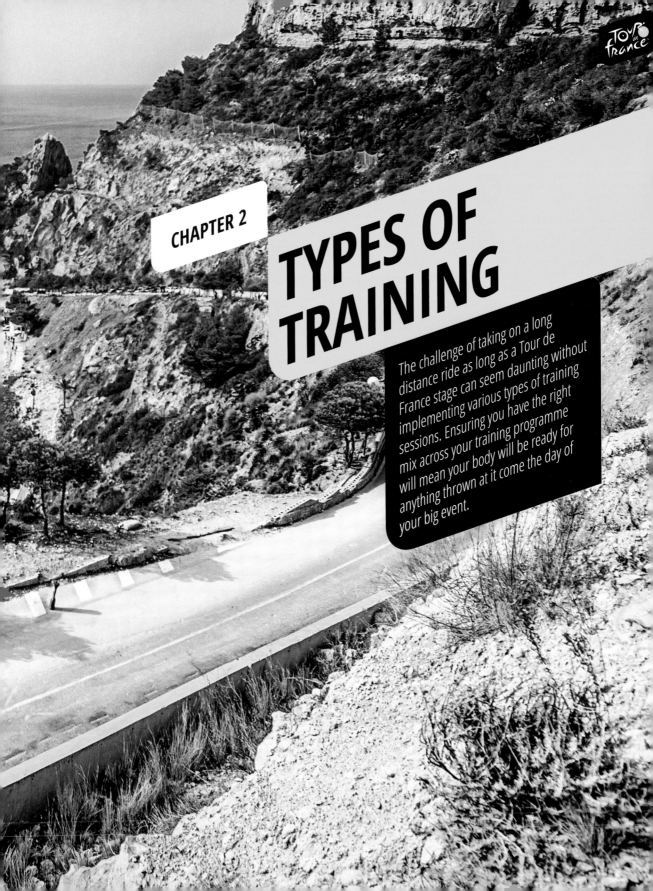

CHAPTER 2

# TYPES OF TRAINING

The challenge of taking on a long distance ride as long as a Tour de France stage can seem daunting without implementing various types of training sessions. Ensuring you have the right mix across your training programme will mean your body will be ready for anything thrown at it come the day of your big event.

# ENDURANCE RIDES

▲ If you want to ride long on your event day, it is key to incorporate endurance rides into your training.

For any road cyclist looking to ride long distances in training, sportives or races, the endurance ride is the bedrock of a training plan. This type of training is also known as aerobic training, and is based around the ability to ride well-oxygenated due to its steady and less intense riding state. Being able to cover long distances and prolonged hours in the saddle will not only train the body to the type of effort required to reach the necessary distances on event days, but also help to train the mind for the challenge and give a sense of respect that riding long distances must deserve.

The chances are you may not have the time in the week to get in rides any longer than a couple of hours, therefore

## ENDURANCE RIDE

The goals of endurance rides are exactly what they say they are: building your aerobic capacity and ultimately your endurance. At times it may purely be down to getting miles into your legs, time on the bike itself and getting the physical and psychological feeling of multiple hours on the bike. But mixing up aerobic rides with tempo efforts can prove beneficial and can replicate increased efforts that will occur during long rides. Just because it may not be an all-out intense effort, beginning and ending your ride with a 20-minute warm-up and cool-down spin is key to ensuring your body is tuned up for the ride ahead and it is also the ideal way to wind down the body before stepping off the bike.

| Minutes | Cadence | Training zone |
|---------|---------|---------------|
| 0–20 | 80 | 1–2 |
| 20–40 | 80–100 | 2 |
| 40–50 | 90–100 | 3-4 |
| 50–70 | 80–100 | 2 |
| 70–80 | 90–100 | 3-4 |
| 80–100 | 80–100 | 2 |
| 60–70 | 80 | 1-2 |

▶ Completing long steady rides in a group can make it far more psychologically manageable.

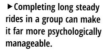

◀ Endurance rides can come to shuddering halt if you don't fuel correctly out on the road.

the weekend provides the best opportunity to hit the road for the longest time. Even though, back in the day, long rides of four to five hours at a low intensity were seen as ideal preparation, the mental and physical sacrifice wouldn't always pay dividends, unless you could supplement these monotonous rides with plenty of varied riding in the week.

Within these long aerobic rides you can also implement tempo efforts if your busy day-to-day schedule dictates it, but they can also be their own rides. These types of sessions or efforts are crucial to long rides, which are broken up with challenging climbs, as it will be the muscular endurance from these repeated climbs that will get you to the finish. This is what tempo efforts build as you ride at a sustainable limit that your body can maintain.

## FUELLING FOR ENDURANCE

Heading out on the bike for any longer than one hour will begin to drain energy systems, and once you go beyond two hours without supplementing your fuel, then endurance rides almost become inefficient in their purpose and you will begin to flag significantly.

Make sure that you have a hearty meal before even clipping into your pedals. Also stock up well with both sufficient hydration – including electrolytes if going out in warm weather – as well as energy gels, bars or natural food that have the right amount of carbohydrates to keep

# TURBO TRAINING

**As much as we would like to ride on the open roads all year round, there are times when staying indoors and hitting the turbo trainer is the wise option. The weather may make road conditions unrideable, or sometimes, the best use of time in our busy day-to-day lives is to complete a time-efficient indoor ride instead.**

▲ Turbo training sessions can be fantastic way of specifying training sessions to the second.

Having this controlled indoor setting also allows you to adapt your session to the individual second, without having to rely on terrain, traffic or weather conditions which can alter specific sessions on the road. To ensure you complete each session at the correct intensity, make sure you carry out initial fitness tests

so each training zone correlates to your personal ability, either through heart rate or functional threshold power. It is also important to retest over time to ensure that your training zones are up to date as your fitness levels – hopefully – improve over time.

## LEG SPEED INTERVALS

Total time: 35 minutes

This session maintains the focus of the physiological response in zones 1–3 whilst, at the same time, building leg speed. Select a gear that will allow you to pedal at 95–110 RPM within the heart-rate parameters for zones 1–3 and don't be afraid to reduce the gearing if your heart-rate is going too high. The workout is made up of two 10-minute intervals with 2½-minutes of rest between each interval. During each interval increase leg speed every two minutes from 95 to 100, 105, 110 and 95 RPM and repeat for the second interval.

| Minutes | Cadence | Training zone |
|---|---|---|
| 0–5 | 90 | 1 |
| 5–7 | 95 | 1-3 |
| 7–9 | 100 | 1-3 |
| 9–11 | 105 | 1-3 |
| 11–13 | 110 | 1-3 |
| 13–15 | 95 | 1-3 |
| 15–17 | 30–90 | 1 |
| 17½–19½ | 95 | 1-3 |
| 19½–21½ | 100 | 1-3 |
| 21½–23½ | 105 | 1-3 |
| 23½– 25½ | 110 | 1-3 |
| 25½–27½ | 95 | 1-3 |
| 27½–35 | 30-90 | 1 |

## TURBO TRAINING TOP TIPS

- Riding indoors can be a sweaty business. With no air resistance or wind to cool you down, it is important to combat it as efficiently as possible. Try to ensure the room is well ventilated and make sure you have a fan set up close by. You should also have a towel close at hand, and taking on plenty of fluids is a smart way to keep cool and hydrated.

- Some days you wake up ready to nail whatever training session is put in front of you; other days can be a bit of a drag. Turbo training sessions can often fall into the latter, therefore having a televison or tablet set up with a TV programme or training videos, such as Sufferfest or Zwift, can help eliminate motivation factors. Alternatively, riding on the turbo alongside a team-mate or friend can help you encourage each other to the end of the session.

- Setting up a turbo trainer on a smooth, solid and level surface limits the amount the turbo trainer moves around needed during sprints and all out efforts, it also helps reduce the noise the turbo sometimes gives out. This not only keeps your family and neighbours happy but also give you full licence to give it your all and go flat out when you really need to.

# INTERVAL TRAINING

▲ Interval sessions may be shorter than endurance rides, but can be just as or more intense.

**Creating a solid base of long miles and multiple-hour rides to work from is, of course, key if your main season goal is completing a long-distance sportive like the *Étape du Tour*. But training all the time at a steady pace over long distances will mean you will never reach a level of training stress that will elicit a performance improvement.**

Therefore, implementing a number of interval sessions into your training plan will not only be key for your physical improvement but also add variety that is crucial to motivation when training regularly. However, be warned, interval training sessions can be very hard work, but

the gains that can be made from the time put in to each session is almost unrivalled to any type of other training in cycling.

The physiological benefits of interval training are clear and include an increase in VO2 max and a reduction in blood-lactate levels, as well as improving peak power and neuro-muscular efficiency. What also makes interval training an attractive proposition is that it can burn fat up to 28.5 per cent more than steady state riding.

The real beauty of interval training sessions is that they can be adapted for whatever type of training effect you are looking to achieve. From micro intervals that are repeated within its own interval, to longer intervals based around a slightly

▶ Interval sessions can be completed at home or out on the open road on the right terrain.

## POWER INTERVALS SESSION

Total time: 60 minutes
Start off this session with a 15-minute warm-up, making sure that the muscles are ready to train at a near maximal effort, ensuring they are warm and loose reduces the risk of causing injuries from high-force efforts. The main session consists of four five-minute intervals, split into one-minute blocks of 20- and 40-second chunks.

During the 20-second effort, ride at a near maximal effort on a hard gear before shifting onto an easier gear for a 40-second recovery chunk at a zone three effort. This 40-second effort should still be completed at a similar cadence, but without pushing the same big gear that was used on the near-maximal effort. It is important to make sure that you have recovered sufficiently to make the most of the 20-second efforts. If you are struggling to recover in time, tweak the efforts into 15- and 45-second chunks.

Once five 20:40-second sets have been completed to make the five-minute interval, complete a five-minute zone two effort to recover for the next interval. Repeat this protocol three more times, before finishing off the session with a ten-minute cool down at a lower cadence and easier gear. This can be completed either on a turbo trainer or out on the road, with the intervals perfect for a shallow gradient or a clear road.

| Time (minutes) | Training zone |
|---|---|
| 0–15 | 1–3 |
| 15–20 | 3–4 |
| 20–25 | 2 |
| 25–30 | 3–4 |
| 30–35 | 3–4 |
| 35–40 | 3–4 |
| 40–45 | 2 |
| 45–50 | 3–4 |
| 50–60 | 1-2 |

longer sustained effort, implementing both into your training will make you a stronger rider over all terrain and circumstances.

With all these benefits from both a time and physiological point of view for cyclists who have time limitations, it is crucial to remember that despite the fitness improvements they can give, long rides must also be completed when targeting a mammoth sportive in the summer months of the year.

# CADENCE

It may seem an almost forgotten aspect of cycling, as turning the pedals is one of the first and most basic skills when we learn to ride a bike. But the speed at which your legs turn, and the subsequent amount of Revolutions Per Minute (RPM) you complete over and over again during a ride can vary how you train and how you tackle varied terrain – especially when it comes to riding in the mountains.

▲ Having the ability to pedal at a range of different cadences can be really beneficial when you ride over different terrains.

In an ideal world, on flat terrain, calm weather and riding at a zone two effort, pedalling around 80–95 RPM is a good starting point for cyclists to aim. This involves finding a gear that is suitable for this cadence rather than forcing the body to pedal at 90 RPM on a gear that you don't believe in, or want to be riding at.

Low cadence efforts of 40–70 RPM may produce high power efforts and be less of a strain on your cardio-vascular system, but can quickly and easily fatigue muscle fibres that are having to turn a big

gear. However, the opposite can be said for high cadence riding, that is above 110 RPM, which shifts the training load onto the cardio-vascular system and is ideal for more prolonged riding.

Finding a balance between the two – while also being able to execute both for short periods – should be the aim for amateur riders. Even though we may have a preferred set cadence that we generally ride at on flat terrain, having the ability to ride at a variety of cadences will really help your riding when the moment requires

you to step out of your favourite zone.

Setting a cadence you want to ride at can also help when pacing your ride. For amateur riders, cycling up climbs will naturally lead to a lowering of cadence. Primarily this allows you to pace your effort for the long ascent ahead. However, as riding at a high cadence for a long time puts an unsustainable and inefficient effort on your heart and lungs to maintain, it is important to keep your effort steady. Even though you may see professional riders effortlessly spinning their way up an ascent, the same tactic may not work for you.

Because the act of pedalling is based around a neuro-muscular motion, having the ability to pedal fast is a useful physiological skill to learn to smooth out your pedalling action. On descents where a higher cadence is easier to maintain, making sure you can actually reach those speeds are critical if you want to gain time and go fast. High cadence drills at a lower power output can be really beneficial for developing your muscles to acquire the ability to pedal at higher RPM's.

Although sticking to your preferred and most efficient cadence is ideal in training, it is also important to listen to your body. When climbing up steep stretches you may need to stand on the pedals to achieve additional power to reach the summit.

▼ Chris Froome and Alberto Contador are legends of the sport but prove that cadence is very individual.

## THERE IS NO ONE SIZE FITS ALL WHEN IT COMES TO CADENCE

Although typically staying within certain cadence ranges can be helpful on a long ride, there is no such thing as the perfect cadence. This is clear in the professional ranks too. Chris Froome is known for pedalling at an extremely high cadence, sitting down when racing and especially when he attacks on a climb. However, one of his biggest rivals over his career was Alberto Contador, who honed his riding by dancing on the pedals, but pedalling at a far lower cadence, especially on climbs. Both are multiple Tour de France and Grand Tour winners, proving that even though there is an ideal RPM range for most riders to pedal at, it won't be the same for everyone.

Mere millimetres can make all the difference during a bike fit.

CHAPTER 3

# BIKE-
# FITTING

You may have been riding for years or just starting out on your cycling journey, but a bike fit is crucial to your efficiency on the bike. It may also keep you injury-free, no matter how many miles you have pedalled in the past. A Visit to a trusted bike fitter may be the best bike-based investment you make, even more than new kit or a bike upgrade.

# WHY, WHERE, HOW?

**You may have heard from riding colleagues or club-mates that a bike-fit is the best investment you can make when it comes to becoming the best cyclist you can be. Even if you want to be just a healthy cyclist seeking a bike-fit, this advice is also applicable to avoid niggles that may lead to long-term injuries.**

There is strong evidence that a bike-fit can benefit both your health and your on-bike performance. We all have unique physical traits and body sizes; this means it is almost impossible that a standard-size, off-the-rack bike will be a perfect fit for your physical make up. This is why a bike-fit becomes one of the most crucial investments a cyclist can make.

▲ Different bike fitters will fit different price points and services: it is key to find one that suits your needs.

### WHY?

If you are looking to increase your time on the bike, then this is the perfect time to get a bike-fit to ensure your set-up is suitable for your personal needs. Even if you have had a bike-fit in the past, if it was a long time ago, or you are splashing out on a new bike, having an expert pair of eyes check your position can be a far wiser purchase – and less costly – than the bike itself.

In an ideal world, if you are thinking of purchasing a new bike, first arranging a bike-fit on a jig may well be a wise investment, This will show a bike that is suited to your flexibility, physical make-up and, ultimately, your riding goals. If a bike-fitter can assess these constraints and provide an optimal position, you will be on the right track for a clean bill of cycling health and – with any luck – increased cycling performance.

### WHERE?

Due to the importance and rise of bike-fitting operators in cycling, there is a plethora of options available, based on your budget and location. It is important to make sure you choose a bike-fitter who has a trustworthy reputation, as there are some who may focus on selling a new piece of equipment rather than the best for your riding ability.

Have an interview with your bike-fitter before you get on the bike. Explain what you are looking to get from your riding, as well as identifying any previous weaknesses or niggles, are key to any bike-fit, so the fitter understands any issues prior to setting you up.

### HOW?

The price of your bike-fit doesn't depend on the quality of the bike-fitter, but probably the equipment they use. From as basic as the eye of a bike-fitter tweaking your set-up on experience alone, to a high-end 3D motion-capture system that is at the other end of spectrum in terms of technology. Both have their benefits, and both can have good and bad results for riders, which can also depend on your budget and what you actually want to gain from a bike-fit. Researching if certain bike-fitters suit your needs better than others can be crucial to saving time and – more importantly – money in the long run.

▼ Bike fits are important for cyclists looking to avoid injuries and niggles as well as improve their efficiency on the bike.

## BIKE-FITTING
# INJURY PREVENTION

▲ Preventing injury is just as important as maintain your fitness levels.

**The saying that claims a "prevention is better than cure" is no more evident than when it comes to a bike-fit. Staying fit and healthy on the bike is often more of a challenge than training itself, and the key to this can be achieved through a trusted bike-fit. Bike frames come in a variety of set sizes, but we are all completely unique in how our body fits onto these frames. Therefore, tweaks are usually necessary to ensure niggling injuries don't lead to time off the bike.**

The most common areas of injury can flare up through bike fits and can range from the top to the bottom of the body. Key pressure areas can lead to common injury trends, typically in the wrists, lower

back, neck and feet. With cycling being a low-impact sport, if you can ensure you stay upright on the road the majority of the time, as well as ensuring you look after these at-risk body parts, your riding should be relatively pain-free throughout the year.

Your lower back is one of the keys areas of your body when cycling. It may not seem to be crucial, as your legs turn the pedals and arms guide you around the corners, but the base to every strong cyclist comes from a strong lower back, and once muscles begin to fatigue around the rest of the body it is the back that picks up the slack. Therefore, having a correct-sized bike frame, saddle height and handlebar position to combat these issues is key.

Another area of the body which is often overlooked by cyclists are the wrists, where

► As one of your key contact points with the bike, your hands and wrists need to be given similar attention set up as the rest of the body.

aches, pains and injuries can all come from poor bike set-up. Putting too much weight and strain through these joints can make cycling unbearable, especially on uneven and bumpy surfaces and this strain can occur from a number of reasons. Setting your saddle up too high will naturally throw your weight forward, as will setting your handlebars too low. Riding a bike that is too big can also leave you stretching out too far and straining your wrists. Despite seeming a small factor, if the brake lever handles are angled incorrectly, and require you to stretch to reach them, your wrists might strain each time you brake.

Once your feet are attached to the pedals, it is often forgotten they are still part of the body, rather than just the transfer point of power through to the pedals. But having pain in the arch or heel can often occur through poorly-fitted shoes or cleat position, or potentially a biomechanical issue further up the body which strains the foot lower down. Buying new cycling shoes when you have a bike-fit may not always be possible, but taking them along to ensure they are the correct size and fit and the cleat set-up is correct for what you require can save a multitude of issues in the future. In some extreme cases you may require insoles to be fitted within the shoes to avoid foot injuries, but this should be seen as a final resort depending on your original bike set-up.

Cycling can lead to the body being put in a number of unusual positions, affecting weight distribution and requiring joints and muscles to be set in unwanted situations for long periods of time. Most affected is the neck, as it is constantly flexed during a ride. This position can be skewed even further by a poor bike-set up and can cause a rider to reach – or hyper-extend – for handlebars that are too far away or too low.

◀ Cleat positioning may seem small but the knock on effect can run all the way up the body.

# BIKE-FITTING
# SADDLE HEIGHT AND SPECIFICATION

▲ Setting your saddle up correctly is one of the key aspects of a bike fit.

**One of the most old-school bike fit hacks that cyclists will carry out is on their saddle. This is not just how the saddle is positioned but also the type of saddle they buy.**

To some it may only seem like the main contact point between the rider and bicycle, but the set-up of your saddle can be crucial for power transfer through the pedals, avoiding knee issues and perhaps the most feared pain of all, discomfort down below.

Identifying the height of the saddle is typically the foundation of any bike fit. Finding the perfect distance between your saddle, handlebars and pedals can lead to so many issues being eliminated almost immediately.

It may be tempting to set your saddle height slightly high, as one of the main downsides of having your saddle too low is that you reduce the potential power output from your leg muscles which can't maintain full extension whilst sitting down. But the height of the saddle is crucial for comfort, which can often be an issue if the saddle is placed too high. This causes your legs to shift from side to side to reach the bottom of the pedal stroke and places unnecessary stress and friction on the contact point of your body and the saddle. It can also lead to muscles and joints over-stretching – having to over-compensate for an extended pedal stroke –

typically in the hamstrings and knees.

It's not just the height of the saddle which is crucial to comfort and performance; the shape, specification and setting can also play a huge role in both of these factors. The width of your "sit-bones" can play a major factor in which saddle works best for you. These hard bones are designed to take your weight, rather than the soft tissue parts – such as muscle, skin and fat – which often lead to saddle sores occurring.

This shouldn't lead you to believe that the softer, most-padded and largest saddle will lead to the most comfort. One glance at the Tour de France peloton will confirm this belief to be untrue. The greater the surface contact area, and more chance of the saddle deforming over time, alongside the potential to cause pressure-point areas, can become a hindrance in the long run for riders.

As a rough guide, flatter and narrower saddles are often used by cyclists who set up in a more aggressive position, while those who are more prone to sitting upright should look for a saddle that is wider and more curved in shape. These are good starting places to think about when purchasing a saddle, as a new bike may come with a high-end saddle, but possibly may not be suit your needs. A bike-fit can help ensure your backside is kept in check, and this means you can stay focused and primed for your peak performance out on the road.

# SADDLE-HEIGHT SETTING HACK

Even though the height of a saddle shouldn't been taken in isolation, sometimes a quick and easy protocol can ensure you start riding in the right ballpark.

• Sit on the saddle, unclip your shoes from the pedals and place your heel in the middle of the pedal axle.

• Turn the pedal to the furthest point so that the crank is in line with the seat tube.

• Ensuring that your hips don't rock to reach the pedal, your leg should be completely straight when the saddle is at the correct height.

• Once this is achieved, clip in and if there is a slight bend at the knee you have found the correct saddle height.

▼ It isn't just about the height of your saddle, the shape and tilt can also have major consequences.

# BIKE-FITTING
# CLEATS

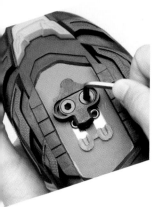

▲ Every rider will have their own preference and requirements when it comes to cleat set up.

**It may be one of the smaller components you buy in your overall kit or bike purchases, but the way you set your cleats up can vary massively. A small tweak in position can prove fruitful all the way up your body as well as ensuring you are getting the full power output from each pedal stroke. An incorrect set-up can equally play havoc with your pedalling efficiency, and can lead to aches and pains cropping up.**

The way you angle your cleat and the fore-aft position of the cleat itself are the two main set up requirements when it comes to fixing the cleat to your shoe. If you angle your cleats incorrectly, then

it is easy to cause pain in your knee or ankle joints from the repetitive nature of pedalling. Setting up your cleats is easy to do yourself, but also they can be tweaked in a bike-fit if you are unsure.

Start off by removing the cleat from your shoe if it is already fixed to it. Put on your shoe as if you were going out for a ride. Locate the ball of one foot and make a small mark on the side of the shoe (or on tape attached to it so it isn't permanently marked) where the centre-point of the ball is, Now repeat the process on the other foot.

Take off your shoes and make a straight line across the sole of the shoe to where the cleat is fixed. Loosely fit the cleat, ensuring it sits on the line with the centre of the pedal axle mark, which is typically

▶ Checking your cleats regularly for wear and tear is key.

found on most cleats. Tighten up all the bolts within the cleat and head out for a spin around the block just to check your shoe isn't rubbing on the crank or causing pain and so needs readjustment.

Another factor you have to take account for is setting up the fore and aft of the cleat. If you ride with your knees quite narrow at the top of your pedal stroke, then rotate the cleats towards the outside of the shoe and the foot inwards. However, if your knees are wide, move the cleats inwards – resulting in the feet moving outwards – which is ideal for a more proficient pedalling technique.

One final basic tweak you can make to your pedals is the tension of the clip itself. When you are first getting used to riding with clipless pedals, adjusting the tension on the pedal itself can be really useful to help you avoid the rite of passage for a beginner cyclist – the slow-motion standing crash that occurs when you forget to unclip coming to a stop. Loosening or tightening the adjuster screw dictates how securely you want to be clipped in, and can be tightened more as you gradually become more confident in your clipping and unclipping technique.

## WHAT CLEATS AND PEDALS ARE RIGHT FOR YOU?

With cleats it is usually personal preference that decide which ones suit you better. Perhaps, most importantly, be sure you don't mix and match pedals with cleats, as different brands only work within their own pedal, despite appearing to look very similar. One of the main differences between cleats is the amount of degrees float they offer, with the major brands ranging from fixed float to nine degrees. Once again, this will be down to personal preference so be sure to experiment to see which one suits you best.

◄ Make sure your choose the correct float in your pedals for your riding ability and personal preference.

Ensuring your energy stores are topped up throughout a ride is crucial to avoid bonking.

**CHAPTER 4**

# NUTRITION

You can plan and execute your training to perfection, but if you fail to fuel and hydrate correctly before, during and after your rides, it can lead to disappointment on the bike and, sometimes – in extreme conditions – catastrophic consequences. Nutrition is an often forgotten part of a cyclist's riding strategy, but it is easy to stay ahead of the game.

# BREAKFAST – THE FUEL TO EVERY CYCLIST'S RIDE

▲ Professional riders need to A smoothie is a great way to get your key nutrients in the morning on the go.

**You can prepare all you want for the ride ahead, nail your training plan, research the route and mentally prepare for what is ahead. However if you aren't fuelled correctly your ride can become more of a struggle than stress-free.**

Nutrition is now such an important area for professional cyclists that it is rare for teams not to have their own chef. Such is the toughness of the Tour de France, riders have to consume as many as 8,000 calories a day just to "break even". This explains teams'

reliance on chefs who know how to whip up vast quantities of nutritious, appetising food, day in, day out.

Breakfast is crucial, as it may have been 12 hours since your last meal, and your body will have used up fuel to repair your muscles and supply glucose to the brain during this time. Even if you think skipping breakfast may help lose weight, the chances are you'll over-indulge later in the day compared to having a good hearty breakfast. If you don't have the luxury of your own personal chef, and in a rush with a busy life, there are plenty of quick breakfasts that can be eaten on the go, the simplest of which is a smoothie.

▶ Team chefs are an essential necessity for each team at the highest level of cycling.

# HOW TO COOK SEAN FOWLER'S GLUTEN-FREE BUCKWHEAT FLOUR PANCAKES...

These gluten-free pancakes are usually a treat or given to riders who need a pick-me-up. This makes eight four-inch – 10cm – pancakes.

**INGREDIENTS:**
2 large eggs
50g olive oil
75g coconut oil (melted)
275ml rice, oat or soy milk
65g yoghurt
125g buckwheat flour
50g rice flour
50g oat flour
1 tsp salt
2 tsp baking powder
½ tsp cinnamon

- Preheat a griddle pan so it is hot enough for water to sputter and bounce when dropped on it.
- Use a small amount of olive oil on the griddle to season.
- Sift all the dry ingredients together in a bowl.
- Mix all the liquid ingredients together in a separate bowl, then combine the two.
- Pour the mixture onto the griddle immediately; it will thicken if it sits for too long.
- If needed, add more rice milk, little by little – but don't overdo it, because the consistency can quickly become too runny.

If you do have time to lay out a breakfast, stay away from the fry-up; eating cereals, oatmeal, muesli, jams, spread and omelettes will provide the necessary nutrients for an amateur rider. Boiled rice for breakfast may not seem very appetizing – and probably isn't necessary for mere mortals – but Mitchelton-Scott's team chef Sean Fowler says 90 per cent of his riders during a Grand Tour chose this option.

"The world of nutrition is a bottomless well of information, interpretations and concepts," he said. "Over the years, I've seen the latest fads come and go: ginger shots, beet shots, kefir smoothies, gluten-free and the rest.

As a team chef since 2009, and an avid cyclist, I have first-hand experience of what works and what doesn't.

"Breakfast should be seven parts carbohydrate to one part protein; for example, a big bowl of oatmeal and then an omelette on the side for protein."

It's not solely about carbs and protein, though; Fowler must ensure that his riders' immune systems and digestion are also looked after. He does this by adding ginger for its antibacterial properties and ensures breakfast soothes his riders' minds.

# ON-THE-BIKE FUELLING

▲ Staying fuelled out the road is key to maintain your optimal cycling performance.

**Stepping onto your bike fully fuelled from a hearty breakfast is the first vital step to a good ride. However, if you are heading out for longer than an hour, you will need to refuel on the open road.**

It may seem a simple tactic but refuelling in the heat of a race or when you a tapping out a solid rhythm on a climb can easily be forgotten and consequently send your refuelling strategy falling by the wayside. Even professional riders can forget to keep their energy stores topped up despite years of cycling, but sticking to a few trusted methods will mean you avoid the dreaded 'bonk'.

There are a number of ways to achieve this and different products, flavours and brands will effect individuals in different ways. When it comes to maintaining energy levels, aiming to consume between 60–90 grams of carbohydrates should be the goal after riding for over an hour. Whether this be through energy drinks, energy gels, bars or natural food itself. Keeping on top of your nutrition by consuming little and often will not only make sure you avoid bonking and allay any fears of digestion issues.

You should base your energy consumption on how you hydrate on the bike, which may have to change depending on the heat and humidity in which you are riding. Using energy drink sachets in one of your two bottles is a good way to stay hydrated and fuelled at the same time; having plain water in the other is always useful, if only to rinse away the sweet taste from other gels and drinks.

**Energy gels** may seem the most unnatural product of them all, stereotyped as sticky and sometimes sickly for cyclists if not used properly, or if an unfortunate explosion upon opening occurs across your bib shorts. However, the development of their flavours, palatability and packaging has improved greatly over the years. Remember though, just because pros discard their used energy gel wrappers at the side of the road when racing, and have them collected by litter-pickers after the peloton has zoomed through, it doesn't mean you can't put yours back in your jersey pocket to keep the world a little tidier.

**Energy bars** are typically more useful earlier in the ride, where you may not be on the main bulk of the climb and your stomach can digest a heavier item of food more easily. Rather than an isotonic energy gel or drink can, the way energy bars are formed nowadays make them taste more like snack bars than a specified energy product.

**Bananas and rice cakes** are still staples of a pro rider's diet on the road. Admittedly, the pros may be more adept at unfolding foil wrappers and consuming the contents on the bike during lulls in racing than amateurs, but if you have the chance to take a quick break and consume some natural goodness, then go for it.

# ISOTONIC, HYPOTONIC AND HYPERTONIC: WHAT ARE THE DIFFERENCES?

**ISOTONIC:** Most traditional sports drinks – such as Gatorade, Powerade, Lucozade Sport – technically fall into the "isotonic" category. This means they are supposedly similar in concentration to human blood, and this means a faster delivery of energy into the bloodstream. Theoretically, they deliver a reasonable amount of energy and clear the gut promptly, too, though not quite as quickly as hypotonic solutions.

**HYPOTONIC:** In simple terms, the fluids in hypotonic drinks tend to be absorbed into the bloodstream the fastest, but they deliver the least amount of carbohydrates per unit volume. This is because hypotonic drinks create a "favourable osmotic gradient" – its concentration is lower than blood, so the water in them flows naturally across the gut wall into blood vessels, moving from an area of lower solute concentration (the gut) to an area of higher concentration (the blood) via osmosis.

**HYPERTONIC:** Hypertonic drinks are more concentrated than your blood. That's because they are usually formulated with lots of carbohydrates to maximise energy delivery to fuel high-intensity activities. Most recovery drinks also fall into this category, with the addition of protein as another major ingredient.

▼ Natural foods such as bananas can be just as effective as energy specific products.

# HYDRATION

▲ Electrolytes tablets are a useful way of ensuring you replace loss salts, with varying contents in each brand.

**Drinking on the bike may seem like an afterthought at times and almost an inevitable action of physical activity, however keeping on top of your hydration can be easily forgotten. If you are riding in a climate or conditions which require additional hydration, it can play a pivotal role in how effective your performance is on the bike.**

Perspiration (sweating) is almost inevitable when cycling for prolonged periods of time, considering the body is made up of 60 per cent water. It is important to replace this, little and often, and as a rough guide a cyclist should look to consume around one 500–750ml bottle of water per one hour of riding on a mild day. However each individual is different so you should adapt your hydration strategy to whatever works best for you out on the road.

Whilst standard water is fine over short distances – less than hour in mild conditions – when the temperature begins to rise, or your ride time increases, then the content of the sweat itself and what is lost becomes more important.

Sweat rates for different people vary, and the salt content within that sweat also varies, so you could have a high sweat rate but low salt content, or a low sweat rate with a high salt content which could affect your performance more. Many hydration companies provide sweat tests so you can find out exactly how your body reacts when the mercury rises.

There are four key nutrients that can affect an individuals cycling performance when it comes to sweat loss. The first of these is calcium, which is vital in conducting signals via nerves for muscle contraction. Second is sodium, which

## HYDRATION DANGERS

Some sports scientists have claimed that whilst striving for optimum performance at the highest level, being slightly dehydrated can help with a rider's power to weight. But this isn't advisable to amateurs, as professionals and their respective sport science teams can measure fluid intake and individual differences far more accurately than the everyday rider. It is also important not to take the replacement of salts to the extreme and over-consume when it isn't necessary. On the flip side, remember electrolyte tablets are typically zero calories, so have zero carbohydrate content. This requires sourcing energy replacement from other methods such as energy drinks, bars or natural food.

# WHAT IS IN OUR SWEAT AND ELECTROLYTE TABLETS

| Electrolyte | Amount lost through sweat | Content within electrolyte tablets |
|---|---|---|
| Calcium | 28mg/l of sweat | 4.8–200mg |
| Potassium | 150 mg/l of sweat | 2.85–600mg |
| Sodium | 230–1,700mg/l of sweat | 200–1,500mg |
| Magnesium | 8.3–14.2mg/l of sweat | 0.36–100mg |

▼ Keeping on top of your hydration needs may seem straight forward, but can easily fall by the wayside over the course of a long ride.

retains fluid and nutrients and maintains cognitive function and keeps blood volume raised. Potassium regulates the flow of fluids and nutrients and counters the effects of sodium to help keep blood pressure levels under control. Lastly, magnesium regulates blood pressure, muscle control and fatigue, all crucial to an individual's performance.

All of these nutrients are plentiful in an everyday balanced diet, but drinking too much water alone can lead to a sodium imbalance in extreme heat. Therefore, mixing in electrolyte tablets is a good way of combating the loss of the imbalance via sweating, but be sure to check the labels, as their content can vary dramatically. It's important to remember there is not one size fits all hydration plan for cyclists, and it should be realised that replacing every single drop of sweat and electrolyte isn't necessary. Replenishing 50 to 70 per cent of losses should be enough to maintain performance. These electrolytes can also be replaced on the bike through other sources, such as energy drinks, bars, gels and natural foods, such as bananas, which are known for being high in potassium.

# RECOVERY MEALS

▲ Alan Murchison is not only a professional chef but also a keen cyclist himself.

**When you step off the bike you may well be tempted to consume anything you set your eyes upon. Typically your body is craving to replace the calories you have left out on the road, but it is crucial to your recovery that you are prepared for the inevitable post-ride hunger kick after you step off the bike.**

After a long ride, a smart way of avoiding unwanted binging is to immediately satisfy your hunger with a protein bar or smoothie prepared before the ride. But you need to be aware of the type of ride you are completing and your subsequent nutrition requirements after a ride are vital. British Cycling chef Alan Murchison explains: "An hour-long ride could be calorie-neutral, or you can go out and absolutely batter yourself and really heavily deplete your energy sources. Make

sure the two are aligned, and you don't over-eat and consume 2,000 calories, because you don't need to do that."

Identifying the differences between the intensities and durations of rides are key for Murchison to plan a refuelling strategy for his riders. As he puts it: "We always say 'everything in moderation', but if you are going to be going out and really hurting yourself, you are going to need protein and carbohydrates. If you look at sports nutrition products on the market, they talk about having 20 grams of protein after a hard ride, which is pretty much spot-on, but having real food as soon as you possibly can is crucial." A three-hour ride for yourself may not require the same nutrition as for a riding mate. So, if you see a friend taking on a protein shake you may not need one, but it depends on the effort you put in to complete the ride.

▶ Recovery meals are key for not only the body but also the mind after a long day in the saddle.

# ALAN MURCHISON'S GLAZED GNOCCHI WITH SPINACH, BROCCOLI, CHICKEN AND TARRAGON

This gnocchi bake is great to have made up in advance to throw in the oven when you have a harder session to do on the bike. We have had this on our menu for British Cycling major events and training for four years now. I really like gnocchi as it is a welcome change to the starchy staples of rice, pasta and potatoes and you can still knock this up in less than 30 minutes.

**INGREDIENTS (SERVES 2):**
500g chicken mini-fillets
500g gluten-free gnocchi
3 teaspoons olive oil
1 broccoli head, chopped
100g chestnut mushrooms
1 bag baby spinach
2 cloves fresh garlic, roughly chopped
100g low-fat cream cheese
100ml single cream
3 tablespoons strong hard cheese (Parmesan or Pecorino)
2 tablespoons fresh tarragon, chopped

1 bunch spring onions, sliced

- Pre-heat the oven to 190°C, heat a large pan of boiling salted water and one sauté pan.
- Cook broccoli up for three minutes and then strain off leaving water in the pan.
- Bring back the water to the boil and cook the gnocchi for 60 seconds, strain off and set aside.
- In the sauté pan, cook spinach over high heat for 60 seconds in one teaspoon of olive oil, season well and press out any excess liquid and set aside.
- Cook the chicken in the same sauté pan for 5–6 minutes with one teaspoon of olive oil, add the garlic, season well and set aside.
- Sauté the mushrooms in the same pan in the last of the olive oil for 2–3 minutes over a high heat and set aside.
- Mix the cream and cream cheese together and season well, add the tarragon into the cream mix.
- Line the bottom of a casserole dish with the spinach, then gnocchi, then broccoli, then chicken and mushrooms. Pour over the cream mix, season and then sprinkle on the three tablespoons of hard strong cheese.
- Put the casserole dish into the pre-heated oven for 20–30 minutes and finish off with the chopped spring onions.

Understanding training data can be key to improving your cycling performance.

THE WOLFPACK

CHAPTER 5

# DECIPHERING DATA

Data is king in today's world. Within cycling, the rise of Strava, TrainingPeaks and other data driven training tools, have become commonplace amongst amateur and professional cyclists alike. However, it is crucial you make sure the data works for you. It should not be just a case of using it for the sake of it, because data can dictate your ride for the worse if it is used in the wrong way.

# DECIPHERING DATA
# WHAT, WHICH, HOW?

Finding a cyclist who doesn't track and record his rides and pore over the data is almost as hard as climbing a mammoth ascent itself. The rise of data within cycling has not only raised the effectiveness of training at the highest level but has made it a useful training weapon for amateurs to take on board as well.

But if you are starting out in the sport, or using data for the first time, you may not quite understand what it is and what it necessarily does. The best way is to explore which types of ride-data analysis works for you is the best way of seeing if it can prove beneficial for your riding.

▲ Having instant feedback on your cycling performance can help you set your training rides to perfection.

## WHAT?

The ride-data collected on a ride can range depending on your recording device. The more common fields include the average, current or top measures of speeds, power output, riding time, metres ascended, cadence, air temperature, heart-rate and distance among many other specific data fields, depending on the device you choose to use and how you set it up.

## WHICH?

There are many ways to record a ride via fitness apps directly themselves, such as Strava or directly on a bike computer, such as Garmin's or Wahoo's. The data from these devices can then be uploaded

▶ Make sure your bike computer and other on bike gadgets are functioning properly before you head out for a ride.

to fitness sites at a later date. For ease of use, phone apps such as Strava, can be ideal for beginners just looking to track the basic GPS data over a ride. A bike computer, however, can be linked with heart-rate monitors and power meters for more detailed and specific riding data.

## HOW?

Once you have completed your ride, you can upload your data to a number of different training websites to analyse your ride. Strava is the market leader, with a number of features, including segments which can show how you perform on a certain section of a ride, such as a climb or an uninterrupted stretch of road. Programmes like TrainingPeaks can give far more detailed analysis about the data itself, with insight into the training zones and power outputs at which your ride was completed, amongst other things.

## DATA DO'S AND DON'TS

**SPEED ISN'T EVERYTHING:** As much as speed is everything, when it comes to riding data, it can actually be a very misleading and often disheartening way of measuring a ride effort. As much as the satisfaction of increasing your average speed, ride after ride, is an obvious way of measuring performance, but this will actually happen very rarely. A number of things can affect this number – including weather, terrain, fatigue and even general traffic flow – so don't get discouraged if the odd ride drops a couple of kilometres per hour every now and then.

**DON'T BECOME OBSESSED WITH THE NUMBERS:** The positives of joining Strava, or another cycling social network, is the encouragement you can get from friends and club-mates, even if you don't ride with them every time you step out on the bike. This can become an obsession at times, if you want to nail certain segments for bragging rights. By all means, there is a time and a place for it, but don't let it come at the sacrifice of your overall training.

**ENCOURAGE OTHERS:** As dangerous as segment-hunting obsessions can be, encouraging your riding mates to succeed and achieve their goals is a great confidence boost when you get home from a long solo ride. Getting kudos from them in return can be the perfect pick-me-up when training seems particularly hard on certain days.

# MAKING IT WORK FOR YOU

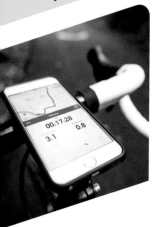

▲ Although data is fascinating and beneficial for your performance, just make sure it doesn't suck the enjoyment out of riding.

**Collating riding data and showing your worth for all to see on Strava, TrainingPeaks or other cycling social media channels is all well and good. But uploading rides just for social brownie points won't guarantee a correlation with improved cycling performance and could be negative to your end goals if not used correctly.**

Looking further into your data, as well as analysing and understanding what it all means, will lead to more efficient training and subsequent physical improvements the next time you are out on the road. Even though a data file may at first be seen as a set of random lines and data points that seem complicated, identifying key markers from each ride can be really helpful for your next training ride.

Despite the vast range of training programme software available, many of them work in the same way when it comes to how they present their data. If you are using a power-meter or a heart-rate monitor then the first number that you will be drawn to – and can tell you something about your ride – is the average power and average heart-rate for your ride. Both of these numbers give a rough but decent idea of just how hard your ride was; if you also track these average numbers over a variety of rides throughout the duration of any given month, then it also gives a good idea of how your fitness levels are developing over a season. The goal of maintaining consistent power, but lower heart-rate, will suggest you are improving your fitness levels.

Observing the line graph of data for power or heart-rate can also show if you have maintained a steady pace throughout a ride. This can be similarly effective if you are aiming to hit certain sprint efforts during a ride, while also discovering if you took sufficient rest in between the sprints. Whether you were able to consistently hit these outputs or heart-rate levels can also tell if your rest intervals were ridden easy enough.

## DATA ISN'T THE BE ALL AND END ALL

Data can tell a rider so much about a cyclist's workload, training and progression. But there is also sometimes a better measure of performance and fatigue and a whole host of other measurable factors and that is your perceived exertion. It may take time but, at the end of the day, you alone will know best what rides tire you out the most, whether you need a rest, or if you feel yourself getting fitter.

If you have pre-set levels based off your Functional Threshold Power (FTP) or Maximum Heart Rate (MHR), then most training platforms will also give a training load or relative effort for each ride. This is ideal for tracking your training plan to ensure you don't over-train on certain rides which may not seem hard at first, but can accumulate fatigue over time.

Data can also give strong indications on just how strong or smartly you are riding as well, particularly on group or mass-participation rides. Comparing data between yourselves and other riders – typically using power data rather than heart-rate data which can be quite personal to that individual – can show just how hard certain riders had to exert on certain sections of a climb. If a rider was able to draft smartly up a climb and then utilise that saved power on the flat, or even when there was little drafting available, it is going to show up in the ride data. Riding smart is often faster than riding hard.

▼ Utilising coaches to interpret your training and racing data can be really useful.

# THE FUTURE OF DATA AND TECHNOLOGY

**The rise and acceptance of technology and data in cycling has become all-encompassing in recent years. With many cyclists feeling naked if they haven't recorded their ride, or head out without their bike computer and phone to share the views they've seen on their ride.**

In all likelihood, this is just the tip of the iceberg for technology within the sport as new developments arrive in coaching and training at the top of the sport each and every season. This will inevitably trickle down to the amateur ranks over time to become commonplace for the everyday rider.

One of the recent developments at the professional end of the sport is the implementation of the computer

▲ Technology has changed the sport over time and will continue to do so.

programme Veloviewer. This has effectively made the traditional road book that each rider, coach and team personnel receive before the race redundant. Veloviewer provides an interactive version of the road book that can be edited to a team's needs on a tablet device that sits within the team car and guides them through the race route as it happens.

The rise of technology is not only helping racing tactics become more sophisticated, it could also be part of road racing itself in the near future. The rise of the virtual training platform Zwift – where cyclists train and race on an online programme via a smart turbo trainer against and with fellow cyclists – has already resulted in national championships taking place in some countries, as well as Zwift racing teams being set up specifically

▶ It may not be long before Grand Tour stages are completed in the virtual world.

for the platform. The rise of the suggestion that a virtual Grand Tour stage could be in the pipeline is no longer a crazy scenario, but a distinct possibility.

The constant striving for the latest and greatest personal technology developments have been spearheaded with cycling teams linking up with other sports striving for the edge in sporting performance. Notably, Team Ineos and Bahrain McLaren have linked up with the Mercedes and McLaren Formula 1 teams, respectively, with Ineos's team principal Sir Dave Brailsford previously researching the use of wearable technology within clothing to track sweat rates, energy expenditure and the subsequent effects it can have on performance.

The swift rise to prominence of the power-meter in recent times suggests the latest technological advancements in the sport may not even be invented yet, but could well change the way cyclists train, recover and race in the near future.

**TEAM SUNWEB COACH MATT WINSTON BELIEVES THE PROGRAMME HAS REVOLUTIONISED RACING TACTICS AT THE TOP LEVEL,**

"It is a massive turning point in how we prepare for a race, it gives you everything, when you have two DS's in the car you can come out of the live section of the programme and go in to the weather app and look at what way the wind is blowing. It is advanced tactics without the need to have local knowledge, In a way it takes away the tactics but it also adds so much and you are at a disadvantage as a team if you don't have it."

Winston believes that programmes like Veloviewer are just another tool for cyclists to venture into the unknown without having to make the trip themselves. "We've just got more technology to use and you can see where the race is going to go and what the race is going to do. In the past you went to Italy and your local DS would know, and the same in each country whereas now everyone is at the similar level."

Mastering the descents after a long climb can be just as crucial to ascending the other side of the mountain.

**CHAPTER 6**

# RIDING EFFICIENTLY

A rider's overall fitness will go a long way to reaching their peak cycling performance, but there are a number of ways cyclists can eke out advantages and save energy along the way through riding efficiently. Just a few tweaks to your positioning in the bunch, reading the road ahead and improving your bike handling skills means you can easily ride more economically.

# DRAFTING

▲ When the peloton puts the hammer down it can reduce the amount of benefits from drafting.

**When watching the Tour de France on television you may wonder why GC leaders such as Chris Froome, and Thibaut Pinot, or sprint kings Caleb Ewan or Peter Sagan, are nowhere to be seen until the crunch point. It is not to stay out of the limelight, but more to stay out of the wind and utilise the effect of drafting.**

This is where the team aspect of cycling comes in to play and is at its most crucial. Even though one person wins the stage each day and only one person can take overall victory in Paris, they wouldn't get there if it wasn't for their team protecting them in the wind – amongst other things – over the three-week race. You may not have a well-drilled team at your disposal, but the

chances are you'll be riding in a peloton from time to time and can still reap the benefits from drafting behind other riders.

Research conducted at the Eindhoven University of Technology ran wind-tunnel tests on a 3D-printed mini peloton of 121 riders, and it showed that riders towards the rear middle of the bunch required only five per cent of the same energy as the front rider to go the same speed.

The energy savings carried out here are extreme and don't bring into account changes in direction or wind, but there are still significant benefits to be made from sitting fifth in line, leading to half the energy required than if you were on the front of the group riding at the same speed.

▶ Staying safe towards the front of the bunch is key for team leaders but staying out of the wind is also key for ensuring energy stores aren't wasted on unnecessary efforts.

# HOW TO DRAFT

The concept of drafting sounds great, but if you aren't confident to latch onto someone's wheel immediately, then you may be a bit worried about crashing into the wheel in front and causing a pile-up in the bunch.

To get better at drafting, start by practising with a friend or team mate on a straight road, and try to ride half a wheel-length behind the front rider, which will allow you time and space to make movements for changes in speed. As you gain confidence at riding at that distance and speed you'll be able to get closer and closer. It is also important not to stare constantly stare at the wheel in front; this can be quite dangerous as you need to be aware of other things on the road. Also, be sure to avoid sudden braking movements when sitting at the front or in the middle of a bunch, but rather feather the brakes to adjust your speed.

Don't forget the wind can also play a role in where you position yourself. Sitting to the left of a rider when the wind is coming from the right and vice versa for the other side are the most efficient ways to draft. But be sure you aren't overlapping wheels when doing this, because it can cause a crash or mishap.

▼ The team time trial discipline is proof for how important drafting can be in cycling.

Riding in a bunch is not all bad for the front rider either, and it is always important to take your turn by rotating positions for optimal speed and efficiency. This same study found out that the front rider even benefited from a small – 3.1 per cent – reduction in wind resistance thanks to a low-pressure air bubble between riders that pushes the leader along.

This data makes it even more incredible to imagine the effort required by breakaway riders to win stages on their own when there is a rampaging peloton using each other's draft to try and catch them before the finish.

# BRAKING

**The act of braking is typically seen by cyclists as purely a way of slowing down and reducing your speed ahead of corners or obstacles in the road. But manipulating your braking – or by braking less though still safely – can actually result in greater returns without extending wasted effort. Of course, braking shouldn't be abused to a dangerous level, but there are a number of ways to improve effectiveness out on the road without needing to make wasteful efforts to get back up to the speed prior to the braking process.**

The act of braking is typically seen by cyclists as purely a way of slowing down and reducing your speed ahead of corners or obstacles in the road. But manipulating your braking – or by braking less though still safely – can actually result in greater returns without extending wasted effort. Of course, braking shouldn't be abused to a dangerous level, but there are a number of ways to improve effectiveness out on the road without needing to make wasteful efforts to get back up to the speed prior to the braking process.

Some riders brake immediately as soon as they see an obstacle up ahead, regardless of the weather conditions, the distance of the obstacle itself or the speed at which they are travelling. Becoming accustomed

► Being smart and feathering your brakes and adjusting speed in small increments is far more efficient for faster and safer deceleration than braking suddenly.

to braking for necessary reasons will mean you don't have to readjust your speed by pedalling again.

There are other options to slowing down when riding on the flat, such as freewheeling and sitting up straight to increase your aerodynamic drag, which slow down the bike's momentum. But these two methods won't be as harsh and won't require as much subsequent additional pedalling to get back up to speed.

▼ Ensuring your brakes are working competently is key for not only performance but also for your peace of mind.

▶ Disc brakes and caliper brakes put out different stopping distances, this is important to realise when riding in a bunch.

## CHECK YOUR BRAKES

Applying the correct techniques is one thing, but if your braking components aren't up to scratch in the first place then you won't see as healthy returns as you could. Make sure you check your brake pads, cables and levers before each ride, not only for wear and tear but also how reliable they are after the previous ride. If they have been worn from a previously wet ride, they may not react as well as when new. Disc brakes and calliper rim brakes also act different, with disc brakes reducing stopping speeds faster and more effectively in wet conditions, whereas calliper rim brakes can be prone to skidding in the rain. Even though disc brakes are better suited to wet conditions they aren't invincible and you should always take caution on wet, gravel or muddy roads as the front brake may not always be your best option on uneven surfaces.

# DESCENDING AT HOME AND IN THE MOUNTAINS

▲ Super tucking may be the done thing for pro cyclists, but can be dangerous if you aren't as skilled or confident.

**For some cyclists descending can be a reward for the hard work of slogging up a climb, whereas for others it can be a bit unnerving, especially if not executed with the right technique and mindset. However good descenders are typically confident descenders who trust their ability as well as their bike to guide them down the mountain in the most effective way possible.**

What is important to remember is that descending massively increases average speed for very little physical effort, so mastering these technical aspects will easily increase your overall speeds. If you're not confident at descending, practicing on local and more well-known roads will eliminate major issues of surprise and can help to build confidence before heading to longer, steeper, faster descents in the Alps or Pyrenees.

It's important to stay relaxed. If you

tighten your shoulders or arms, it can lead to jerky steering or braking motions, which can prove problematic when travelling at greater speeds. However, tentative movements potentially can cause issues at the other end of the spectrum.

When descending, unless you are properly pushing a big gear on a shallow descent, you probably won't need to pedal as much as normal, if at all. Therefore, shifting your leg position and body weight when cornering allows for a smoother ride. Bending the knee that is going around the inside of the corner, and straightening and putting your weight through your outside leg means you should distribute it evenly around a bend.

Even if you are nervous don't drag on the brakes. It may be tempting to drift down a climb, constantly hunkering on the brakes, but it is not the most efficient way of riding – or helpful for your bike's health either. It may not only wear out the brake pads if you are riding with calliper brakes but also, in extreme circumstances, could cause a tyre to overheat and blow out.

## BEWARE OF THE SUPER TUCK

The rise of the "super tuck" within the pro peloton recently has been shown during live coverage of the biggest races. This is when riders have sought to attack on the downhill or make it back into the bunch having been distanced on the climb. However, sitting on the top tube of the bike doesn't always mean faster and certainly not safer speeds. Leave it to the pros and make sure you master the basic skills to reap the rewards.

Scrubbing speed off before you reach a corner is the most efficient way to manage a descent, before, during and after the corner itself. Braking in the corner can lead to the brakes locking up, which can lead to the wheels sweeping out from underneath you and falling off.

Descending at speed also requires being aerodynamic; so positioning your hands on the drops and getting down low reduces the wind resistance that can slow you down. Consequently, sitting up is a very useful air brake if you want to naturally slow down more gradually then slamming on the brakes.

Going faster downhill may require less physical strain, but increased psychological awareness of what is happening around you and on the road. Spotting the turn early, being aware of possible road obstacles and focusing on your position can buy you time, before locating the vanishing point, whilst going around the corner will lead to taking the fastest and safest line through the bend.

▼ Mastering your descending skills will mean you increase your average speed without needing to improve your fitness levels.

# THE IMPORTANCE OF AERODYNAMICS

▲ The use of wind tunnels are key for professionals to hone their position, but for mere mortals a few simple tricks and tips can reduce your drag.

**The use of aerodynamics may only be seen as relevant for time trialists or Formula 1 junkies. However, for anyone looking to go faster on the bike, getting aero is the best way to get a little extra free speed, rather than weight-loss or increasing your power output. In fact, slower riders will actually see bigger gains from becoming more aerodynamic on the bike than those at the top end of the sport.**

Air resistance is the primary resistive force when riding a bike, with the frontal area of your body and your bike accounting for 80–90 per cent of your total resistance when riding on a flat road.

It is only when a climb rises above five per cent gradient that weight becomes the overriding resistance factor. This is why professional riders and teams spend hours in wind tunnels tweaking and perfecting their positions and techniques. However, this may not be time-efficient or cost-effective for an amateur rider, but there are a number of other methods which are far easier and cheaper.

One of the most basic techniques – one that is often overlooked because of its simplicity – is riding on the dropped handlebars rather than the tops. Riding on the tops may not even be done intentionally, but riding on the drops can reduce your aerodynamic drag by 20 per

► Chris Froome may not look aero going uphill, but is a demon descender thanks to his aerodynamic positioning.

cent compared to riding on the brake hoods or on the top of the handlebars.

Tucking in your elbows can also save valuable watts. It may not be the technique that has led Chris Froome to multiple Grand Tour wins but for mere mortals it cuts down the aerodynamic drag that little bit more. Shrugging your shoulders and tucking down your head will also help reduce your frontal area even further.

One aero tip that requires zero physical effort is the kit you wear. This doesn't mean buying the latest aerodynamic skin-

suits on the market – although if you want to get the ultimate aero benefits it is very efficient – but even just a couple of well-fitting jerseys and jackets slice away the drag. If you aren't too keen on a figure-hugging look, even just keeping your jersey and jacket zipped up, rather than flapping in the wind, will help.

Applying just a few of these methods will hopefully see you cut through the air that little bit smoother and faster, saving energy and increasing your speed on the road.

## DEVELOP AN AERO BODY

Maintaining an aerodynamic position requires being flexible and having good core strength. These stretches and exercises will set you on the right road to achieving both.

### THE PLANK
Completing isometric exercises will not only build your core strength, but also replicate the position on the bike that you need to hold when on the drops. The plank is held in a similar position to that of a press-up, but with your forearms being the contact point with the ground instead of your hands. Hold the body in a position so a straight line from your feet up to your head is formed. Hold for 45 seconds, increasing or decreasing the time depending on your ability, and repeat three times.

### STRETCH THOSE HAMSTRINGS
Hamstrings are the muscles that are most prone to tightness due to the shortening action that occurs when pedalling. Bend over at the waist and gently ease your arms down towards your toes, maintaining slightly bent knees. Hold for 20 seconds and repeat three times to help improve your flexibility.

### ELIMINATE YOUR LOWER BACK ISSUES
One of most basic exercises to help reduce your back pain is the prayer position stretch. Lie on your front with your knees bent up against your torso, reach out with both arms stretching your fingers as far as they can go. Try to keep your bottom stretched back, towards your feet, hold for 20–30 seconds and repeat three times.

Tapping into the brains of more experienced cycling aficionados can reap great rewards.

**CHAPTER 7**

# WORDS OF WISDOM

It may not seem like it, but cycling is more of a team sport than meets the eye. Even though individual riders take the glory, there is no rider in history who would be able to succeed without the help of their team out of the road and behind the scenes. Setting training plans, receiving tactical advice out on the road and ensuring their nutrition is on point are just some of the services elite riders crave from their team.

# MATT WINSTON, TEAM SUNWEB COACH

▲ Before joining Team Sunweb, Winston was part of the British Cycling junior set up before a head coach role at ONE Pro Cycling.

**The way Sunweb is we don't officially have any sports directors within teams but we have coaches. If you take a step back and take away the old school cycling mantra, we are very much not an old school team, because our job is to coach riders through the races. Give them the tactics but also review it with them and talk about how we can do it better and then go forward. The people who do the physical part are called trainers who train the riders to be in top shape and then we coach the guys to race and hopefully get the best out of themselves for the team and of course we drive the team car and hand out bottles which for Team Sunweb was probably the smallest element. If you want to just be a Director Sportive by driving a car and handing out bottles then Sunweb definitely isn't the place for that. I also coach eight of the guys in the team, we have six coaches in the WorldTour team and four are personal coaches, so the riders are allocated to each of us and we are their point of communication, they talk to their trainer a bit about the training but we are their point of communication for everything.**

Course preparation is key, even at Sunweb we ask the riders to come to the race with the course prepared. There is an expectation that they aren't just looking at us who gives them all the information. We expect them to come to the race, knowing the course, knowing where the climbs are, their fuelling strategy, so they know when they are going to eat and drink during the race so they've already got a plan. Its just little things to help with the preparation, if you are set on going for a target time in the Etape du Tour, knowing the length of a climb, and your ability to climb an ascent in a certain time. You can work out where can to make up time that puts yourself in the positive rather than losing time. If I was riding I would aim to ride at 32kph on the flat, then if I can ride a little easier on the climbs or if you have got a strong climber who can make up time on the climbs rather than the flat, you can actually make the biggest gains by looking at the course and actually plan where you can expend the most energy rather than going in to it too fast. Which is easy to do if you've never done it before and you are excited, but taking a moment to consider the course and make notes on your stem can be really beneficial.

I think the biggest tactics are pacing, your nutrition strategy and parcours information are the three things that may move you from a bronze time to a silver time or a silver to a gold. Because if you get those wrong then you are losing maybe a minute a kilometre to what you normally would. You can really turn it around by having that background to it and its something that everyone can do as well. It doesn't matter if you are an elite rider or getting on the bike for the first time. Everyone can look at where they are going, everyone can eat and drink on a bike and everyone can pace themselves, once they've done a few rides and got the feel for it. It sounds so easy but even the pros get it wrong, the pros don't pace themselves and crack on a mountain or they don't eat and it just shows how easy it is to get it wrong. They do take a lot of work to get it right, and you may get it wrong the 11th time after getting it right the first ten times and think what is going on.

◄ Winston is a key cog in Team Sunweb's tactical and coaching set up.

## WORDS OF WISDOM

# KOEN PELGRIM, DECEUNINCK QUICK-STEP COACH

▲ Pelgrim is integral to co-ordinating training, testing and performance analysis across the Belgian team.

▶ Rarely seen at races, Pelgrim is a vital cog during pre-season camps and training throughout the season.

**I think at the moment, and the way that cycling has developed in previous years, most coaches – or a lot of them in the pro peloton – have a physiology or sports science background. So I think that is something really special, but of course that background helps you understand the training process, understand how the human body works and reacts and how you should interpret certain strategies or new things that come along into the sport. So, for sure, it's helpful to have that background to give you that little bit extra.**

Every day is different in my role, so there is no such thing as a classic day-to-day role. If you are at the training camp, you are busy with the practical side. We have 28 riders and it is more of a practical thing organising plans and training, dividing groups and talking to riders, whereas at home, its more office based, and I make programmes, receive training data files from the riders and process them. Then, of course, during the season, you are always busy preparing upcoming training camps and keeping up to date reading up on the latest science.

It is very important that riders like what they do. It is almost as important as making training programmes as good and efficient as possible, because, at the end of the day, riders are humans and not machines, so you have to motivate them also.

When it gets to the race itself, my job should be done but, of course, it is always important to stay connected with the riders and the team when they are racing because that is what it is all about. You have to keep in contact with the riders, and see if things are going as planned, or if anything has gone wrong in the period before, or if anything hasn't gone as planned, so you can adapt your programme for the period after the race. But you've also got to keep in contact with the riders as well, because you are a coach. It's not just a case of making a training programme, you have to have a close relationship with the riders as well. It's not as though they go to race and you say, 'my job is done, see you in two weeks.'

I think the most important thing for amateurs is to keep listening to their body. A training programme is important, but it consists of doing the right training and getting the right amount of rest. Sometimes you have riders who hear so many things nowadays that they get lost in the details if they have to do intervals of eight minutes or ten minutes, or they have to do a certain amount of hours or something. Or they may always be crunching the data when they get their power meter out but, at the end of it, the basics are still to do the right amount of training at the right amount of time. If you get that balance right, then you get 80 to 90 per cent of the thing correct and the rest builds on that. If you want to get to the highest level, these small details should not take you away from the basics. This still is the most important thing, and can make the biggest difference.

# ALAN MURCHISON, BRITISH CYCLING CHEF

▲ Murchison is a big believer in that nutrition isn't just important for professional riders but for amateurs as well.

**I cover all the major events for British Cycling, from World Road championships, Track World Cups to the European Track Championships, making sure we provide solutions and food for all the cyclists pre-, during and post-competition and they have exactly what they need to recover for racing and training. I also work with the performance team to look at the schedule to organise a menu that works for the guys that is also signed off by the team's Performance Nutritionist.**

Every event and every rider will have slightly different requirements: the sprinters could be at the track for two hours, or could be there all day and late into the evening, depending on how they get on in each round. So it's not uncommon for them to race six times in a day, for multiple days. But they have confidence to come to me at 4.00 pm, asking for some porridge, or something completely different.

One of the key factors in this job is having the ability to go into a hotel kitchen in completely new surroundings and deliver. You could be serving breakfast at 5.00 am, and still be there at 11.00 pm making dinner. They are very long days, but it is good that they have the confidence to come and ask for whatever they want.

The other thing is being on the same page as the athletes. They may get back to the hotel after racing all day and can't

stomach food because they are full of caffeine and sugar and absolutely buzzing. Sometimes they may come to you and have a smoothie at 11.00 pm, because that's all they can actually stomach. If you've been battered riding a Madison, or a sprint, then a full meal isn't right, but they still need something inside them. I've never come across an athlete who finishes a really hard training ride or race and says, 'you know what I really need: 20 grams of protein.' They just want to eat, but if you can make it interesting and appetizing, and also fit for purpose, that is what matters.

Many amateur riders want to get round Grand Fondos feeling fit and strong and ahead of their mates, and without the right nutrition it just isn't possible. Nobody who has ridden a bike so far has said they want to go slower. Everyone wants to go faster, and I think food is as important as any part of the performance make up, and anyone who thinks they can go out and train for four hours on a bottle of water and a banana is kidding themselves. If you think how much money does it cost to lose a kilogram of weight off your bike, if you have a 9 Kg road bike to get that down to seven will cost you thousands of pounds. But to lose two kilograms off yourself is a really easy performance gain. There is not an athlete out there – with the exception of a couple –who can't find a couple of kilograms to lose on their body and that is a really easy performance gain.

The other thing riders need to look into is what have they done the day before, and what have they done the day after. It is a cumulative effect of fatigue that is going to get you. If you have gone out for a two-hour easy ride, that can be really hard if you have done three 30-minute blocks at sweet-spot. Suddenly that two-hour ride isn't as easy any more. If you then add on a hard session the following day, then that becomes a very different thing altogether, as you could still be fatigued or tired.

▼ From Grand Fondos to Grand Tours, staying well fuelled is key.

# WORDS OF WISDOM

# LISA NIJBROEK, TEAM SUNWEB NUTRITIONIST

▲ Nijbroek has been with Team Sunweb for three years including an unplanned stint as the team chef at the Giro d'Italia.

"Nutrition is really important, because what we see in pro cycling is that the races are four, five or even six hours long, which means the riders have to drink extra because they probably only have 1½ hours of fuel already in their body, but then it becomes really important they start eating. If they don't eat anything after 1½ hours of exercise, and it is the same for an amateur rider, then they will lack in energy and pretty soon they will have to step out of the race and not continue. Especially in pro cycling, when you have a multiple-day race of seven days – or even the Grand Tours of three weeks in row – then nutrition is a really important role within that.

We have three full-time nutritionists in the team, and I am more responsible for the overall plans so I have two colleagues who work with the athletes themselves, but it varies throughout the season. In January, we start with basic menus for the home situation and then the intensity isn"t too high because they have just started training. Then, during the season, we adapt the plan for each race and have different plans for a stage race than we would for a one-day race, so we guide them and have a call with them each month and, with some riders, every couple of weeks by message or a phone call, just to talk about the last details before going into a race.

I think one really important thing for amateur riders is that they practice with sports nutrition at home, or in a training situation, before they start using it in such a race or competition. I see quite often with amateur riders they grab a mixture of gels, bars and isotonic drinks and they actually have no idea what they are doing, or how much they should take. They may not have tried it in a training situation, and your stomach needs to get used to the amount of carbohydrates and sugars that you are taking during a ride. One really important thing, when preparing for such a long ride, is to train with a sports nutritionist in a training situation, so they know how the body will react or if they have stomach complaints. Another important thing is the timing of the last meal before going into such an intense ride. Normally we always advise our pros to take their last big meal three hours before going on the bike, which is mainly down to prevent stomach complaints or reduce the risk of stomach complaints to as low as possible. If you take a big meal an hour before going on the bike, the body is still digesting it and it is likely you may have complaints during the ride. It's quite long in between but this is when eating a big meal, so it's not a case of overeating, but about 1½ hours before riding, I would suggest a small snack of a muesli bar or a piece of fruit or a rice cake.

During the Grand Tours, especially we see that challenge come through of keeping the food interesting, because the race is three weeks long and the riders are away for four weeks because we leave a couple of days before the first race day starts. The highest expenditure I've seen in a day was 10,000 calories on a mountain stage, so it is almost impossible to eat all those calories again within the same day and it's a really big challenge. Then, in the last week, we see riders can have difficulties because it is the hardest, with mountain stages and they have difficulties with eating enough.

We always send a menu upfront to all the riders and ask them what can be motivation food for the final week. This may be things like tiramisu or pizza, and we try to adapt it to make it as healthy as possible. Or, sometimes, we make a pie for dessert, but with oatmeal and a middle layer of fruit so it looks like a pie. They may see a pie on the plate, but it's quark with oatmeal, and it is all really healthy and because it looks different, it can be really motivating for them.

▼ Staying on top of your nutrition and avoiding guilty pleasures when training can be easier said than done.

Being able to drink, remove clothing and change gears effectively will guard against any bike handling mishaps.

CHAPTER 8

# BIKE HANDLING

Improving your bodys engine and your mental stamina are just a couple of aspects of becoming a complete bike rider. If you can ensure that your bike handling skills are in check you will not only see your performances improve but also increase your feeling of safety on the bike as well as the safety for other riders out on the road.

# ETIQUETTE AND SAFETY

▲ Riding in traffic on the open road may seem daunting but knowing the do's and don'ts can make it less intimidating.

**Staying safe out on the open road can be a hurdle that most amateur cyclists are wary of crossing when increasing their riding output. One of the main issues can be riding in traffic as it often brings trepidation for many, but it doesn't need to if you are sensible with your road positioning and understand which signals to use when riding with a group of other cyclists or on your own.**

Hiding in the gutter may seem safe, but actually a driver is less likely to see you and it gives you little room to manoeuvre from potholes or drain covers which are typically at the side of the road.

Another smart move when planning a training route is to avoid major junctions and busy roads if possible. This not only will make the ride more free-flowing and require less stopping and starting on your ride, but also will also make it more enjoyable as you aren't breathing in the fumes of cars waiting to pass through traffic. Although filtering is often safer, it is also important to be wary of filtering through traffic if it is not safe to do so. Sometimes it is safer to stay further back in the line of traffic at a red light if it is about to turn green.

It may seem small, but ensuring that you keep your bike fully maintained will give you the peace of mind that it won't let you down when you need it most. This isn't a case of buying the latest and greatest upgrades for your steed, but ensuring that your tyres, brakes and gears are all fully functioning will ensure that you can react to what happens on the road accordingly, and the bike can react in good time as well. This will also give you the psychological peace of mind that you aren't a mechanical fault away from a major mishap.

▶ Being safe in the bunch is crucial for not only your safety but for every rider around.

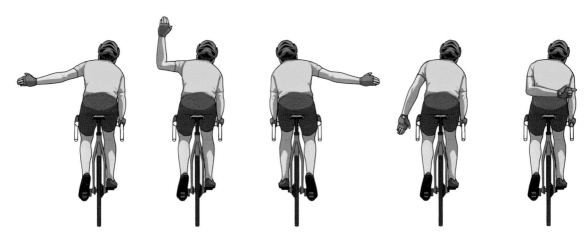

# RIDING SIGNALS

Riding in a group is a great way to feel safer on the road. Making sure you are more visible to other road users will mean that they should take more caution when approaching or overtaking you if the group is riding in the correct manner. But you can help each other – and other road users – by using hand signals and communicating you or the group's intentions. Here a few top tips that all cyclists should know:

### TURNING

Clearly raising an outstretched arm sideways at a 90-degree angle allows your group and other road users know that you are turning left or right. It is important the arm is fully outstretched at this angle so as not to confuse with the signal to point out obstacles in the road lower down.

### MOVING LEFT OR RIGHT

This is used when there is an obstacle at the side of the road encroaching on the current line you or the group are taking – often a parked car or a horse – and you have to move out from the side of a road. Place a hand on the base of the back pointing in the direction to which the group needs to move.

### POTHOLE/DRAIN COVERS

Pointing down towards the obstacle in the road will let riders behind know if they need to move slightly to the left or right of the road to avoid it depending on their location in the group. If possible, calling out to other cyclists what the obstacle is can also be helpful.

▲ Using hand signals are an excellent way of letting other cyclists and road users of your intentions.

# GEARING

▲ Don't be afraid to change your set up depending on the terrain you are riding.

One aspect of your cycling performance can be affected before you even swing your leg over the saddle. When it comes to gearing, most cyclists just stick to what came with their bike and go from there. However, there are alternatives that can be far better suited to your fitness levels and the terrain you plan to tackle.

First of all, let's explain how your gears work. Your front gears are the chainrings, or the crankset, which sits next to your right crank arm, these make big shifts in gears when changing them, and the bigger the chainring the more power is required to turn it. Your rear gears consist of the cassette, which sits on the back wheel, and these make far more incremental shifts when changed. In these cases, however, the bigger the cassette the less power is required to turn it.

Adapting your group sets for the type of road riding you are doing can be useful when heading into the high mountains. These mechanical or electronic gearing

group sets typically come in standard (53 x 39-tooth chainrings), compact (50 x 34), semi-compact (52 x 36) or triple (50 x 39 x 30). The typical rear cassettes that are fitted onto road bikes range from an 11- to a 25-tooth chain ring, giving you a decent range for most European terrain but may not be as efficient when in the high mountain ranges of the Alps of Pyrenees. A compact or semi-compact group set is commonplace for most amateur riders nowadays and even professionals drop down to these group sets on high mountain stages. A standard group set may well be adequate if you live on flat terrain, but when you head to the mountains it is rare to hear a cyclist complain their gears were too easy. It is more than likely they will say they wish they had just one more gear to help them up that final climb.

The main skill when using gears come from preparing for what is coming up the road ahead, and changing gears before you hit the change itself. For example you may be flying down a descent which then hits a very

## CROSS-CHAINING

Whilst there may be some occasions where it is hard to avoid it, cross-chaining is something that all cyclists should be wary of doing for long periods of time. This is when the chain is forced to stretch across from the big front ring to the big rear cassette or vice versa from the small chain ring to the small rear cassette. It is not only less efficient but can put significant stress on your drivetrain, and this can wear down vital components.

steep uphill section. Anticipating this change in gradient, and adjusting gears accordingly, will save effort, maintain speed and keep your bike's components flowing, compared to changing gear on the climb itself.

It is also key when riding in traffic to shift to an easier gear when coming to a stop at a red traffic light. By flicking down the gears, you aren't pushing a massive cog when the light turns green and it means you will get away from the lights more smoothly and safely.

Lastly, it is far more efficient to maintain a constant, steady power through the pedals with consistent pedalling, rather than grinding a big gear at a cadence of 40–60 RPM along and perhaps coasting every ten pedals strokes because the strain on your muscles can't handle the load. Spinning an easier gear and maintaining a cadence around 80–100 RPM is more efficient for prolonged riding as it shifts the effort onto your cardio-vascular system – ideal for endurance rides.

▼ Professional riders need to have a good hearty breakfast on the morning of every race day. Keeping your gears in check can be crucial to ensuring they don't fail at the key moment of a race or ride.

# ON-BIKE SKILLS

▲ Being able to drink and eat on the go cannot be ignored.

**Riding a bike is something the majority of us take for granted once we learn the basics from a young age. But actually honing these skills is a never-ending process to become faster, safer and more efficient on the bike.**

In the pursuit of improving your cycling performance it is common that bike-handling skills are often neglected at the expense of fitness gains, and whilst they are important, prioritising them, and sacrificing them ahead of technical development, can limit the upper end of your potential.

There are a few drills that can be done and even just a few minutes before each ride can see significant improvements out on the road. One of these effective drills for bike handling is the "car-parking trick", where you simply attempt to complete a 180-degree turn within a parking space without going over the lines. Focusing on where you need to go will help you make the turn; repeating this in the other direction will help develop your braking, speed and turning judgement.

Another drill can be completed on your morning commute to perfect your balance on the bike. As you approach a red light, slow down to ride as slowly as possible – when it is safe to do so – whilst maintaining your balance before the light the turns green. This drill doesn't develop

into standing at the lights itself, but it is the first step to eventually mastering that ability.

These drills are key for balance and speed control of the bike, but there are some skills which may not directly make you faster, but can be taken for granted if not executed. Another major but often overlooked skill is riding a bike one-handed, this isn't just so you can wave at your friends out on the road, but to carry out actions that are required during long sustained riding.

This may be from taking your drink out of a bottle cage to rehydrate, or reaching for an energy gel or banana out of your jersey pocket. Both require maintaining control with one hand still on the handlebars, whilst staying in a straight line going forward and covering the brakes in case you need to stop or slow down whilst eating. It is also wise not to reach for a drink on a twisting descent, in crosswinds or slippery roads where conditions can be changeable and require full attention and complete control of the bike. If you are struggling to open energy bars once you have located them in your pocket, slightly opening the top of the packet before you start your ride is a smart idea. This ensures you can eat them quickly and have both hands back on the handlebars as quickly as possible.

These abilities are based primarily around balance and using a technique that works best for you. Whether this is using a certain hand, technique or grip for one thing and a separate one for another, or placing your drinks and food in places which are easier to reach than others. Whatever works best for you, it is important to ensure you can carry on drinking and eating with confidence.

It is not a case of everyone learning and mastering these proficiencies at the same rate, so do be patient when learning and developing your bike-handling skills; they can require time and perseverance through regular training in a variety of situations. Even the best cyclists in the world will develop their skills to adapt to ever-changing aspects of their riding and racing.

▼ As your skills advance, carrying out actions such as removing clothing in the bunch will become second nature.

Even pro cyclists need to relax and recuperate to ensure they perform at their best.

**CHAPTER 9**

# REST AND RECOVERY

There is a saying that claims, "your next ride begins, as soon as you step off the bike". In many ways this is true. The way your body recovers is not only crucial in making sure you are ready for your next ride, but also can play a valuable role in your body's ability to make physiological improvements that occur when recuperating.

# AVOIDING INJURY

▲ Utilising a foam roller after a ride or training session can help alleviate any ongoing niggles.

**Road cycling can be a brutal sport at times, pushing the body and mind to the limit on a couple of skinny wheels with just some lycra protecting our body from the tarmac below. Obviously, there are risks involved when crashing, but it is usually an avoidable act and, when you consider the non-contact and low-impact nature of the sport, cycling is actually a relatively safe activity and low-risk in terms of injuries.**

However, there may be a time when you are forced off the bike because of a few niggles and knocks that are regularly picked up by cyclists, but these can be avoided. If you can prevent them from occurring in the first place, you'll be a far better cyclist for it. Remember, a niggle in one part of the body can lead to a knock-on effect elsewhere.

One of the most common areas for injuries come in the lower back. It is hardly a surprise, considering the positions cyclists hold for hours on end, and it can also shorten hip flexors. Another factor is that many cyclists also have sedentary jobs, such as staring at computer screens, then it almost seems inevitable that physical issues present themselves.

Implementing a few core-strength exercises will help to reduce the chance of your lower back collapsing on the bike, adding to the strain. If you stretch out your back and hips with a foam roller after each

ride it will also help to alleviate flexibility issues. If this doesn't solve it, there could be there are issues of over-extending your handlebar reach, and this can be cured with a bike fit.

Knees are another problem area for cyclists, and these typically can come from saddle issues. This may be from being set up too low, and placing undue stress on the patella, or from being too high, which might cause pain behind the knee as the hamstrings compensate by stretching to complete the pedal rotation. Cleat-position and set-up can also have a knock-on effect on the lateral and medial areas of the knee as it doesn't track correctly. Whereas taping the joints and muscles, and making adjustments to bike components can help initially, long-term cures will result around loosening the IT (iliotibial) band – the tendon which goes down the outer thigh between the ilium (pelvis) and tibia (shin).

As previously mentioned when it comes to injuries, there can be a knock-on effect to the body – none more so than the wrists, arms, hands and neck being interlinked when it comes to injuries. The majority of the time these injuries are traced to handlebar-reach, height, angle or compression of the hands at an unnatural angle. Sourcing a bike-fit can help alleviate these – and many other issues – as well as wearing padded cycling gloves to minimise numbness that can occur in the hands and fingers.

Lastly, and most delicately, one issue

that cannot be avoided is saddle sores. They may not be a discussion topic for the dinner table, but they can cause serious discomfort and have even forced pro riders out of races when they become unbearable. Trying to sit lop-sided can cause other injuries further down the body when compensating for saddle sores. It is crucial the area is kept clean and dry. If it hurts to ride with the sores, then a few days off the bike is a must to ensure the initially outbreak calms down.

To prevent them from coming back, you should finding a saddle that is specific to your needs. It will also help to get some well-fitted cycling shorts with chamois cream as this can help reduce friction and kill off bacteria. As tempting as it may be to lounge about in sweaty kit after a ride, changing out of bib shorts and showering straight after a ride is vital if you want to eliminate the growth of bacteria.

▼ Stretching before or after a ride is key to stretching the body out of the closed motion of cycling.

# MEASURING FATIGUE

▲ Spotting the signs of fatigue can sometimes be tricky.

Unfortunately from time to time there may be cases where your body or mind can't go any further, whether it is from over-training or the stresses of combining a riding programme with the pressures of day-to-day life. Fatigue can cover many different bases, it isn't just from one ride where you may have pushed yourself to the limit and felt tired at the end of it. It is the process of feeling physically or mentally drained during the early stages of a ride or before you have even stepped on the bike itself.

Of course, you need to push your body to make fitness and form improvements, but rest and recovery periods are just as crucial to achieving peak performance. Just as importantly, if training is starting to hamper your health off the bike, then it is time to realise your limits. In extreme cases, fatigue can be caused by Over Training Syndrome (OTS), but other signs can also point to the need for a prolonged rest off the bike.

One of these is if your heart-rate is notably elevated when resting, in comparison to your baseline heart-rate when fit. In some cases it may even be suppressed; either way, any major changes

▶ Analysing training data can help see which sessions or training weeks have been particularly heavy going.

may call for a rest off the bike. Another sign is a disruption in sleeping patterns – or even insomnia itself – and this is notable because when training regularly sleep should seem consistent, but in times of over-training it can have an impact. If a rider loses their appetite, given how cyclists tend to enjoy a snack or two on and off the bike, then this should be an easy sign to spot.

Be aware not to attribute just one of these signs on one single day to feeling fatigued. We all have bad days on the bike, can pick up illnesses and have injuries from other sources. It is critical to make sure you spot fatigue before it can truly impact your training, but don't let it give you the fear of training itself.

## MEASURING FATIGUE THROUGH TRAINING DATA

Although fatigue can sometimes build up over time, training data from power-meters can give a clear – and, more importantly – early sign to a rider they may be physically peaking in form or in need of a rest. These four data signs are key to discovering just that.

### TRAINING STRESS SCORE (TSS)
This number relates to the intensity of a single training session with higher numbers showing when it has been more strenuous.

### ACUTE TRAINING LOAD (ATL)
This is a short-term fatigue number that is accumulated and estimated over a seven-day period.

### CHRONIC TRAINING LOAD (CTL)
This longer-term fitness accumulation rating is based over a 42-day period. More recently-completed rides are weighted higher towards this number.

### TRAINING-STRESS BALANCE (TSB)
This number is the difference between CTL and ATL and displays if a rider may be approaching top form. When the number is positive, it indicates a good performance is approaching after a decent block of training combined with a low recent value of fatigue. This number should show when tapering before a target event has reached optimum level.

# POST-RIDE DIET

▲ Sourcing natural forms of protein can be key to ensuring your muscles recover sufficiently for the next ride.

**As soon as you finish a training ride, the temptation may well be to relax on the sofa and binge-eat back the hard-earned calories you had burned off out on the road. But even though these culinary treats may sooth your mind, it is a crucial time for the body to recover through nutrition and this is the point of a post-ride diet.**

One of the key nutrition areas that every cyclist should target after a ride is their protein intake. It may have been seen as something only body-builders needed to load up on, but protein is vital for repairing and rebuilding damaged muscle fibres

that occur when exercising. The process of muscle protein synthesis is the driving force behind the body's adaptive response to exercise, so it is crucial if you don't want your muscles aching for days after each ride and to see and feel the gains you deserve from your training.

The recommended protein intake for adults is 0.75 grams of protein per kilogram of body weight, per day, but this is just for the everyday person, living a normal daily life. For cyclists, consuming 1.2 to 1.5 grams of protein per kilogram of body weight per day is required at a minimum for weight maintenance.

Just like when you are on the bike, a grazing method of little and often is better

▶ Recovery shakes are an ideal way to beat that hunger pang immediately after a ride.

than trying to consume hefty chunks of protein in single sittings. Your body can't process large amounts of protein at once, so eating three massive steaks 30 minutes after a ride isn't going to hit your protein goals for the day. The timing of what you eat is just as crucial as eating smartly and ensuring what you consume is appropriate. On days when you are recovering, feel free to lower your carbohydrate intake as your energy needs won't be as high as usual, but you will need to increase your protein intake to repair muscle fibres.

Your protein options don't have to be limited because of your dietary requirements, and Greek yoghurt and eggs are excellent alternatives for vegetarians as opposed to the traditional fish, red or white meats. Vegans can look to tofu, soybeans and nuts as fine sources of protein.

Even though natural food is better for the body, mind and soul, sometimes a quick and convenient blast of protein is required if you don't have time to cook a meal. Protein supplements can come in shake or, more recently, gel form to get the necessary protein requirements. These are ideal to have immediately after a ride, can be pre-made, and consumed before showering, then eating a proper recovery meal an hour or so after your ride.

Whereas protein is key for recovery, there are other macro- and micro-nutrients that cyclists should aim to consume after a ride. Carbohydrates may not be as important in recovery as when fuelling your ride, but you will still have a deficit post-ride that needs replenishing. In this case, pasta or rice to supplement your protein is ideal as these two major food groups provide that vitamins and minerals that can stave off illnesses that come when the body is at its weakest.

## NUTRITION DO'S AND DON'TS

- Low carbohydrate diets may be the current trend in weight loss, but remember carbohydrates are your main source of energy. This is particularly crucial in cold weather where glycogen depletion can be accelerated.

- Supplementing your diet with vitamin D is more vital in the winter due to reduced exposure to the sun. Vitamin D is needed to keep your immune system ticking over to help prevent illnesses.

- Another area of nutrition that should be observed is balancing your acid-base metabolism. High levels of acid within the body can make you more susceptible to infections. Avoiding white flour, dairy products and refined sugars can be very beneficial towards achieving this.

# COOL-DOWN TECHNIQUES

It is almost normal to see cyclists partake in warm-ups before every type of ride they do. Even amateurs have become more and more accustomed to replicating their pro counterparts by conducting a structured warm-up. Research has showed if a warm-up is not done, it can have a significantly negative effect on your performance.

Cool-downs have traditionally been

forgotten in road cycling and cycling teams have only recently adopted them after gruelling Tour de France stages. It may only take a small amount of time to complete, they but can be crucial to your body's recovery for the next ride by returning the body to its pre-exercise state.

Conducted in almost an opposite intensity trend to the warm-up, the cool-down should get progressively less intense as the body gradually adapts to returning to its pre-exercise state. A good

▲ Despite how much you have drunk on the bike, replenishing fluids is key when you are cooling down.

▶ Cooling down isn't all about taking a nice refreshing dip.

cool-down should involve maintaining a moderately-increased heart-rate for 10 minutes to allow the stabilisation of pH balance within the muscles. Focusing on pushing a high cadence, rather than grinding a bigger gear, is also key.

Because of the repetitive fixed movement that cycling incurs for long periods of time, it is also important to stretch and mobilise the main joints of the body after a ride. This includes the ankles, knees, hips and back, focusing on both the joints and surrounding muscles.

There may be occasions where you do not go straight home after a ride, and have to sit in a car immediately after a ride. Going from one fixed position on the bike to a different fixed position in a car, train or even a plane can be problematic. Hip flexors and hamstrings are prone to shortening during prolonged sitting positions, and this may not only lead to muscle soreness on the following days after a ride but also can have a limiting effect on power output and aerodynamic positioning in future cycling performances as well.

You should try to remobilise the muscles and joints during a long journey with stretching or walking, by taking regular rest stops, or even utilising foam rollers, massage balls or massage sticks. All of these can help to break up the monotony of prolonged stationary travel.

## KEY COOL-DOWN TECHNIQUES

- Wearing compression garments can help promote recovery, and can be worn to clear the build-up of toxins and promote blood-flow after each ride. These can be ideal if you have to travel immediately after a ride and sit still in a car for a prolonged time.

- Carrying out cool-down protocols after each ride is crucial and, just because it was a short ride, it doesn't mean your body won't feel fatigued and achey the following day.

- Cool-downs should be gentle enough that you can consume food and drink to help aid recovery. A nutrition supplement, such as a protein recovery shake, water or an electrolyte drink, all help the recovery process and can be done on the bike or in between stretching.

▲ The cafe ride can be the most enjoyable but critical part of a training week.

**Rest days aren't always about lying horizontally on a sofa counting down the hours until your next ride. Even though these are required from time to time, active recovery is key to keeping your body and mind ticking over.**

One of the main aspects of active recovery is the recovery ride. This may be seen on the surface as additional mileage on top of a hard session – as it is often when they take place. However, recovery rides should be taken at a far reduced intensity and time, both of which will help the body continue to keep ticking over rather than shutting down completely. This will be noticeable during your next intense training session, when you should be able to hit higher intensities far quicker than if you had rested completely.

One way many riders at both the professional and amateur levels incorporate this into their schedule is through a café ride. One of the most social aspects of

cycling is heading out for a coffee at a leisurely pace and on comfortable terrain, riding easily enough so you can hold a conversation along the way. This isn't to say that heading out for a solo recovery ride is useless; admittedly, you won't be tempted to ride at the same pace or tempo as your ride partner, but you can fully focus on your needs. Just be sure not to over-indulge at the café once you reach it.

Choosing a flat and short route that is preferably shorter than an hour 's riding time but not longer than 1½ hours is ideal. These rides are also a good time to work on your cadence, as you should be riding them in your lowest gears to limit the stress on your muscles. Don't get these recovery rides confused with short intense sessions that you may have in your training programme. Despite being similar in lengths of time, they must be ridden at their set intensities to get the full benefits from each.

It may be tempting to leave your bike

## OVER-TRAINING WARNING

Whereas active recovery works for some people, sometimes it is too much for others, regardless of how low the level of intensity is that they complete it. Whether it is depleting energy sources further or adding undue stress to lingering injuries or illnesses, sometimes it is best to stay off the bike and away from all physical activity. Remember, training plans and sessions should be adaptable to your own personal well-being and training progress.

computer at home when enjoying your recovery ride and not showcase your sluggish ride to the world online. But keeping it close to hand is worthwhile, despite not necessarily hitting any personal bests on the road. Make sure you keep your heart-rate, power-output and effort-levels under control and within the recovery ride boundaries so you don't overdo it when you don't need to. You might find taking an older winter bike for a spin will eliminate any internal temptations that your speedy number one bike may offer you subconsciously.

Even though the recovery ride is one of the main active recuperative sessions you can carry out, there are other ways to achieve this through other sports such as running, swimming or even walking the dogs. Anything that can slowly raise your heart-rate and help keep you moving is ideal for a lighter day's training.

▼ A social ride can be just as important for team building.

# SLEEP

▲ Don't take sleep for granted, as it is a secret weapon when it comes to recovery.

**Even though it takes up almost one-third of every single person's day, sleep is pretty much ignored or at least a forgotten recovery technique by cyclists and athletes, even though it is their main day-to-day recovery weapon. Sleep is key to the body's recovery off the bike, but it is often seen as an afterthought and sacrificed in busy day-to-day lives.**

The importance of a regular, uninterrupted night's sleep has been taken so seriously at the pro level by Team Ineos that in Grand Tours they've taken their own mattresses and pillows to replace the hotel options so their riders have a consistent sleep on the same mattresses day in, day out, regardless of their location. They even trialled the idea of riders sleeping in motorhomes during stage races, but this was banned by the UCI, the sport's governing body.

Sleep may be more important, night after night, for the elite competing in multi-day events, but it is still an underused factor in the recovery for amateur riders as well. Understanding your sleep cycles, sleep patterns and circadian rhythms can help the body recover fully – both mentally and physically. Whether this is through adopting regular sleep routines and understanding your chronotype, it means you can adapt your training schedule accordingly. Even sleeping for one hour longer on weekends can upset your body's biological clock and make it harder to readjust back into a normal day-to-day

▶ Ensuring your home is set up for perfect sleeping conditions is more than just a comfy bed.

sleep pattern.

The time of day you exercise also may affect your sleeping patterns. A late night ride may seem the perfect recipe to tire out the body for a decent night's sleep, but the adrenaline of the ride may instead keep you awake for hours afterwards.

The amount of sleep required is also dependent on your individual needs. The often-mentioned number of eight hours of sleep is, more accurately, an average of the spectrum of the recommended sleep, which is between seven and nine hours. Taking a midday nap may also be appealing but it is important not to make this the equivalent of a second stint of sleep; instead use it as a top-up to your main sleep at night. Also, be aware, sleeping beyond three or four o'clock in the afternoon will have negative implications for your sleep that evening.

## TUNING YOUR BEDROOM INTO A SLEEP HAVEN

There are a number of things you can do ensure you have an immaculate night's sleep. Your food and drink intake prior to bed can have a direct effect on your sleeping patterns. For instance taking things like caffeine and alcohol are well known to adversely affect your sleep, whereas perhaps less well-known foods rich in melatonin – such as bananas and oatmeal – can help a peaceful night's rest.

Room temperatures can play a crucial role and influence the length and quality of your sleep and the optimal temperature of your bedroom should be kept around 18°C. A room that is too cold or too warm can both have detrimental effects to a settled night's sleep, as can a room that is too light or too noisy. Buying black-out blinds to block out light, or wearing an eye mask, as well as combating noise with earplugs can help to overcome these issues.

A more recent trend and issue has been the use of electronic screens before sleep and even in bed itself. Tablets, laptops and phones give out high levels of light, and using them immediately before bed can interfere with melatonin production. Reducing this altogether, or ensuring your devices are fitted with software that can adapt the screen to the lighting conditions, will help reduce these subsequent issues.

It's not all about the bike, when you can improve off it.

CHAPTER 10

# OFF THE BIKE TRAINING

Putting in the hard yards on the bike is, of course, crucial to improving your cycling ability, but carrying out some training off the bike isn't just for the elite riders. A few tweaks to your training programme, and adding some gym sessions that are specified to cycling can really help boost your performance, as well as keep any lingering niggles that will hamper your short- and long-term health at bay.

# WEIGHT TRAINING

**The obsession of road cyclists being light, lean and lowering their power to weight ratio has often put off amateur cyclists from hitting the gym and lifting weights. However, the obsession with power and watts lies in the name right there, half of the "increasing your power to weight ratio" mantra means becoming more powerful.**

Strength training can often bring a grimace to the face of most cyclists, with the majority thinking that spending any spare time lifting iron in the gym, compared to turning the pedals on the bike unthinkable. However, implementing just a few simple strength-training routines into your weekly plan can provide significant performance benefits, which can't be achieved as easily out on the open road or on an indoor trainer.

If you want to get stronger on the bike then you have to adapt the way you are currently training. A number of scientific studies prove that one of the main reasons off-the-bike strength training can improve bike-specific strength qualities, is through the neurological adaptations that occur, rather than just the sole increase in muscle mass.

Of course, if you are really strapped for time, then sacrificing a session on the bike for the gym when you only have a couple of slots in a week may not be useful for your personal programme. It may well be likely that you go to the gym already within your week, but don't utilise cycling-specific workout exercises. or execute the correct sets or reps to properly enhance your cycling performance. Therefore, dropping the sets and reps down in your workouts to focus on more maximal efforts which increase strength and maximal load training, shouldn't then have a negative impact on your on-bike training.

Strength training is a different stimulus altogether, and it will evoke a slightly different response and slightly different neural adaptations that you won't get unless you actually complete them. These exercises don't have to be anything complicated to bring about long-term benefits, simply completing the basic exercises well can help achieve these goals.

▲ Working through different movements will make the body stronger overall.

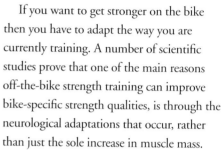

◀ It is key for cyclists to have a strong core to transfer power through the pedals.

# NOVICE TRAINING PLAN – ONE-HOUR SESSION

This is a basic-level conditioning session that establishes strength-training work with a few main exercises and some additional supplementary work. Regardless of your cycling fitness, if you have limited strength-training experience, it is crucial to prepare the body and address weaknesses in the same way you would training a beginner to cycle.

| Exercise | Sets x repetitions | Rest between repetitions | Notes (Increase weight in steady increments each week depending on progress) |
|---|---|---|---|
| Leg press | 3 x 8 | 90 seconds | Start at 45-degree angle and don't lock knees out when legs are fully extended. |
| Hamstring curl | 3 x 8 | 90 seconds | Can be achieved on a standing or lying down machine. |
| Single leg hip-thrust | 2 x 15 | 30–60 seconds | No additional weight, keep shoulders in contact with floor. |
| Lat pulldown | 2 x 15 | 30–60 seconds | Narrow grip on cable machine. |
| Side plank | 3 x 30 seconds | 30–60 seconds | Allow and elbow or hand to be the contact point with the ground. |
| Dead bug | 3 x 16 | 30–60 seconds | Lift and lower opposite arms and legs. |

◄ Training together with friends or family can keep your motivation levels high.

# CROSS TRAINING

**If the monotony of regular cycling training is affecting your psychological wellbeing, then a dose of cross-training may well kick-start your enthusiasm once again. Typically, you may well implement this during the winter months of the off-season, when the weather is less appealing, or if you have no immediate goals on the cards. But a short mid-season break, or throwing in the odd cross-training session into your normal training week, will help mix things up and keep you mentally refreshed.**

The first port of call for most cyclists who fancy a bout of cross-training is running. Some cyclists feel that even a mention of the sport is blasphemous, but it comes with many benefits if planned out and conducted in the correct way.

Firstly, due to the high-impact nature of the sport, it is important to wear some decent and supportive running shoes. It's not a case of going out and buying the latest release from the Nike factory, as the chances are you won't be using them all that often. But it is vital that what you are running in can help protect your cycling joints and muscles that may not be used to the impact of running. Quite simply, the trainers you've had in your cupboard for the last ten years probably aren't going to do the trick.

It's not just the shoes you wear that will make the transfer to running easier on your body, running off road on grass or dirt tracks will also limit these effects that can cause Delayed Onset Muscle Soreness (DOMS) during the days afterwards. If you are short on time, running can be an excellent time-efficient replacement compared to the bike and also more enjoyable in poor weather.

Implementing running into your week will also help increase your body's bone-density levels, which can be limited when cycling due to its non-weight-bearing tendencies. As previously mentioned, take it easy for your first few runs as your cardiovascular levels may be stronger than what your muscles and joints can cope with.

Whereas running possesses dangers of stereotypical high-impact injuries, the complete opposite can be said for swimming. Taking a dip in the pool for a recovery session – or a full-on cardiovascular workout – is a great way of keeping your training from stagnating. The weightless workout is perfect for cyclists who can also utilise breathing techniques to further their fitness.

One of the benefits of swimming is that you can also focus on working your upper body, which may be neglected on the bike, with your legs doing minimal, but still notable work. The passing of water over your muscles has a therapeutic effect as well.

▲ Running off road or on trails can be a far better transition for muscles and joints.

# THREE OTHER CROSS-TRAINING ALTERNATIVES

### CROSS-COUNTRY SKIING
It may not be particularly accessible to the majority of cyclists but, arguably, it is the best cardiovascular workout you can adhere to. Working the entire body, as well as having zero impact on your bones, muscles and joints – barring any crashes – cross-country skiing is often a go-to activity for pro cyclists in the off season.

### HIKING
Embracing the great outdoors, and ascending to mountain tops on your two feet rather than two wheels, may be exactly what you are after. It also helps to maintain your key cycling muscles, glutes, quads and hamstrings to name a few.

### YOGA/PILATES
The physical and psychological benefits of yoga and Pilates are notable as they not only improve your strength, flexibility and focus to benefit your wellbeing on the bike but also it can almost be done in any location.

▼ Cross training isn't just constructive for the body but also the mind.

# YOGA AND PILATES

▲ Being flexible is a key attribute for any cyclist.

**Many may have sniffed at yoga and Pilates as a fad by over the years, but it has been a growing trend across many sports, and has been crucial to keeping athletes finely tuned both mentally and physically. Cycling is no different, with a wide range of professional teams and riders now adopting both kinds of protocol to enhance their bodies and minds.**

The act of cycling and the closed and restrictive movement on the bicycle is unique to the sport. Whilst it may not bring the impact dangers to muscles and joints compared to running, it can limit every day movements which, in turn, causes niggles that can affect your riding ability.

During the action of cycling, certain joints and muscles move within one range of motion, with the repetitive motion leaving other muscles and joints that aren't used as much or taken through their full range of motion, imbalanced as a result.

This can lead to shortened or tight hamstrings and hip flexors, more impact on the shoulders, neck and back, rounding of the shoulders and a shortening of the pectoral muscles. For example, stretching the lower back is a great antidote for the forward-leaning flexed position on the bike. By cyclists stretching their hamstrings in a balanced way, they will be able to increase their range of motion when pedalling and reduce the level of injury. This can be done within many of the yoga postures.

For amateurs, the day-to-day working life of sitting in an office chair can also cause poor posture in the back and hips, and this only accentuates the need for off-the-bike care.

Regular yoga and Pilates sessions can see an increased flexibility, elongate tightened muscles, increase core strength, balance muscles, improve breathing and body awareness, as well as providing a clarity of mind which results in improved cycling performance and a reduction in the risk of injuries.

The premise of Pilates, in particular, focuses on core strength and balance, which plays a massive role, not only in a cyclist's performance and power transfer through the body into the pedals but also in having a strong base.

This can help to alleviate other potential niggle points, such as the knees which aren't compensating for weaknesses during strenuous efforts on two wheels.

# THREE YOGA POSTURES FOR CYCLISTS

Here are three cycling specific yoga exercises that target the muscles and joints of cyclists to keep your body ticking over:

### DOWNWARD-FACING DOG
An all-round good posture to do for cyclists which strengthens medial deltoids, biceps and triceps. It also increases upper-body strength and balances out the effects of the cyclist's handlebar-grip and the rounding of the shoulders or pressure on the lower back by stretching out the erector spinae, latissimus dorsi and pectorals. It also stretches out the hamstring and glutes.

### SINGLE-LEG FORWARD BEND
This posture gives you a stronger stretch in the hamstrings, whilst also stretching the hips, spine and calves, with your legs and core strengthened at the same time. Additionally, it can help relieve stiffness in the hips, shoulders and spine. Be patient and use breathing to ease gently into the posture especially when dealing with tightness in the body.

### COBBLER'S POSE
This seated posture stretches adductors, strengthens core abdominal and back muscles and opens the hips. It helps to relieve sacroiliac pain and discomfort and reduces sciatic pain.

◄ Introducing yoga or pilates into your week can pay dividends on the bike.

The team on the road is just a small part of the entire team's make up.

# HOW THE PROS PREPARE

What works for professional riders may not always work for amateur cyclists. However, tapping into the minds and wisdom of some of the world's best cyclists and coaches can show just how they dedicate their lives and what they sacrifice in training to stay at the top of the sport.

# THE TEAM BEHIND THE TEAM

▲ Being the voice in the riders head can be a big task for the Directeur Sportif.

**What you see on TV – when a rider takes a stage victory or puts on the yellow jersey at the end of the Tour de France – is far from an individual effort. Behind the glory of one person is a success shared amongst their team-mates and the hard work put in behind the scenes by the backroom staff.**

Although some teams have different titles or job structures for certain roles, a rider who doesn't have the support of a team which covers the majority of these bases won't be able to function to their full capability and succeed out on the open road.

## DIRECTEUR SPORTIF (SPORTS DIRECTOR)

Often one of the senior management team, the DS will be in the team car behind the race, speaking to the riders over the radio, issuing tactics, race updates, warnings about the road ahead and often general encouragement. They may also coach individual riders depending on the team.

## COACH

The coach may have a larger role in tactics in some teams more than in others, as well as being assigned to individual riders within the team itself. This may be structuring training plans for the season, as well as assisting with individual sessions and reconnaissance training camps to climbs that are set to feature in upcoming races.

▶ There is so much more to the team than the riders out on the road.

## CHEF

Rarely being seen at either the start or finish of a stage doesn't mean the chef doesn't play a massive role in the team, as they are always ahead of the race preparing the evening meal for the riders, as well as the breakfasts for the following days. Early starts and late finishes are the norm in the life of a head chef for a cycling team.

## PRESS OFFICER

This person manages all the media requests for the team, be it television, radio, written press or online media. They are often seen lingering in the background when riders are being interviewed after a stage. When a rider is leading a race it is likely they could be spending most of their time with the press officer, fulfilling duties that come when holding the *maillot jaune* or other race-leading jerseys.

## SOIGNEUR

If there is a job role that requires a true all-rounder, then the *soigneur* (which translates as therapist or care provider) is just that. From preparing feed-bags in the morning and heading out to the feed-zone for the race as it zooms past, to organising laundry for the team and giving riders a well-earned post-race massage. A *soigneur's* work is often the most time-consuming and varied in the sport.

## MECHANIC

Mechanics are responsible for all of the team bikes, ensuring they are running smoothly and cleaned after each stage. As well as catering for individual preferences, such as chain sets, saddle heights and tyre

choices, they will often sit in the rear seat of the team car with a spare wheel and tools needed for quick repairs after mechanical incidents that may occur out on the road.

## BUS DRIVER

Driving an 18-tonne bus up and down mountains, across a wide range of countries, is just the tip of the iceberg for the team bus drivers. Aside from ensuring the cycling team's haven is kept in good condition, they are also one of the go-to members when a rider needs a pick-me-up if morale is low.

▼ Soigneurs have to be on their guard during the hectic feed zones.

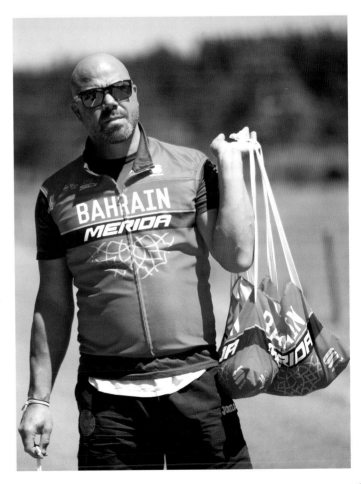

# WEEK IN TRAINING, MITCHELL DOCKER, EF PRO CYCLING

▲ Docker has racked up thousands of miles over his career, so knows what is required for him to perform.

**The training week for a professional rider can vary greatly depending on their upcoming goals, from building a base for the season ahead, building high-power efforts for the classics or tapering for three-week Grand Tours. Australian rider Mitchell Docker described his final 30½-hour training week before the start of the season.**

### MONDAY - ENDURANCE RIDE (FIVE HOURS)

"My week started with a five-hour endurance ride. I was training in the Macedon Ranges, about 70 kilometres north-west of Melbourne. This week was my last build-up week before the season, with an 'all-in' attitude to get the last bit of base training in. Then I start freshening up and start racing the following week at the Tour Down Under, before going across to Europe and it is about race recovery for a big chunk of the season."

### TUESDAY - ZONE FIVE EFFORTS (SIX HOURS)

"This was a six-hour day and I touched into some zone five efforts. Over the ride I accumulated 12 minutes within zone five which is a race-intensity level effort. I can do that whatever length I want – a one-minute effort, a ten-second effort – whenever I see an opportunity up a hill to accumulate that 12-minute amount over a six-hour ride."

▶ The Australian is a key part of EF Pro Cycling team.

## WEDNESDAY – ENDURANCE RIDE (FIVE HOURS)

"On these endurance rides, ideally you don't want to be jumping up into any threshold efforts, because they are just about ticking over. This for me is zone two and making sure I'm just getting the endurance in and waiting for the more specific days to get those harder efforts in. It is also just trying to accumulate the time for the week as well, so you don't necessarily have to do anything special on these days and I was maintaining my heart rate at 140bpm."

## THURSDAY – RECOVERY RIDE (1½ HOURS)

"With a couple of kids and a family now, it is key to get that balance. When I do go out on recovery days, I put emphasis on those rides. This week, the days after my recovery days were important effort days, so it was important I still felt I rolled out after the hard big days and could get into those efforts straight away after the first ten minutes or half-hour of the ride. These recovery rides have a purpose, but on some days it is purely a recovery day."

## FRIDAY – ONE-MINUTE EFFORTS (5½ HOURS)

"In the first hour, I completed five one-minute efforts to reach that top-end level, and helped to deplete the system a bit. This was because the whole aim of the ride was to get to 4,000 kilojoules, which is what we burn on a race day. Once I reached that level, I produced a ten-minute race effort, and this was at the five-hour mark. Some days it's personal-best power, on others it isn't anything special from a power point of view, but it is down to perceived effort. If it feels hard, then it is hard and it doesn't matter what the power is. At the end of the race you don't care if you are setting a PB if you don't win, as long as you win that's what it's all about."

## SATURDAY – RECOVERY DAY (0 HOURS)

"Sometimes it is important just to have a day off the bike so you are physically not in that position and psychologically for me it is huge too. Some people don't need that, they just love being on the bike riding down to the coffee shop and meeting other people. I do understand this and sometimes do it too, but its that time with the family and work that I have to do, rather than do it for passion. If I can have a day with the family, it's much more important than going out there for the sake of it."

## SUNDAY – TEMPO, ENDURANCE AND ABOVE-THRESHOLD EFFORTS (7½ HOURS)

"My last day of the week was a big 7½-hour day. It started off with a two-hour tempo effort, just sitting below threshold. I followed this with three hours of endurance riding, before the 1½ hours, which included eight four-minute efforts with four minutes of recovery just above threshold at 400 watts. I was doing them at about 440 watts, and I then rode home to build up the time to 7½ hours, just to push an extra 30 minutes to close the door on the preseason and know it was all in the bank."

# DIET IN A DAY, ADAM HANSEN, LOTTO SOUDAL

▲ Adam Hansen is one of several vegan riders to race in the pro peloton.

**The diet of a pro cyclist can generally be described as sizeable. Ensuring that all the necessary nutritional needs are covered is key for a rider to fuel sufficiently and recover for the following days racing. No cyclist knows this better than Lotto Soudal's Adam Hansen who rode a staggering 20 grand tours in a row. The Australian rider goes through his daily vegan-based diet.**

### BREAKFAST

"I would like to think my diet is far more specific compared to non-vegan diets because I don't have the extra non-important food groups. For example, I would eat what everyone else eats for breakfast for a typical big day on the bike, mainly oat-based, some muesli or porridge. We have All-Nuts as a sponsor, so we always have dried figs and dates, which is great for making it sweet and also bananas are my favourite to add. If you want to, you could also have pasta or rice. I don't, but some riders have jam on toast or bread. I try and stay away from processed foods, and I include bread in that because of the refined flour, and the sugar in jam.

"So, all of this is vegan and very carb-based, which is the ideal breakfast for any athlete. The difference between my breakfast and others, is would have cheese and ham on bread – like a lot of Germans – or some eggs. However, these have a high fat content by themselves or how they are cooked and they only slow down the digestion. Also, there is no benefit of having protein before a big race. Protein is over-consumed throughout the day, and only should be taken when required."

### PRE-STAGE

I would snack before a stage, because we have a maximal intake of about 90grams an hour of carbs and I try to start that just before the start of the race so I don't fall behind. Some riders wait a full hour into the race, but that is an hour they lose throughout the race to catch up. This isn't possible, because we burn far more than we can digest. For me this can be an energy bar, banana or even rice on the bus before."

### DURING AND AFTER THE STAGE

"During the race, I have only energy gels and all gels are vegan, so that is pretty straightforward. After the race, I have a special sugar drink from SANAS our sponsor. This is to replace glycogen in our system and create an insulin spike. At this period, you are at your most anabolic state, and I take a vegan-based protein shake which is normally a pea, brown rice or corn-mixture version. You have to take a mix of different types, instead of just from one source, because all nine essential branch-chain amino acids need to come from a balanced vegan diet.

"New research has found that there is no limit on plant-based protein to human health and for this reason, I can consume a lot more and don't have problems with my kidneys. I can have far more and recover at a better rate. This is what I believe helped me during all those grand tours."

### POST-RACE MEAL

"After about 15 minutes, I will have a high-carb meal to refill glycogen stores and help speed up recovery before the next stage. It may be potatoes, rice, pasta or even oats again, depending on what's on the bus. We also have a wide choice of beans, legumes, and lentils, which are a great balance source of everything we need, including complete proteins for recovery. Also, the extra green leafy vegetables mean I have some healthy fibre

to slowly release carbohydrates and have very stable blood-sugar levels as opposed to during the race, when I'm only eating sugars that do the opposite."

### DINNER

"I have some roasted veggies that are provided by our team chef. There are always so many options, and I mix them with nuts, beans and legumes again, and there is always pasta or rice. I am more of a rice fan, because it's less processed. Other meat-eating cyclists might have chicken or steak at night, and have sauces made from animal products. I think sauces are one of the worst things to add because, at certain hotels, they can have extra amounts of sugar or fat added. If it has been a really hard day, I would also have a protein shake before going to bed."

◀ The Australian had to stayed well fuelled during his record breaking 20 consecutive Grand Tour rides.

# THE IMPORTANCE OF POWER TO WEIGHT

▲ Achieving your optimal power to weight ratio is key to crushing the climbs.

**It may be a phrase you have heard riders, coaches and commentators talk about every time the Tour de France heads into the high mountains. But the importance of a rider's power to weight ratio cannot be underestimated. Despite the hype, the sum to calculate this magic number that all pro riders strive to increase is simply the amount of watts a rider can put out in comparison to the their body weight in kilograms.**

Finding the balance of riding at the lowest weight, but producing the highest amount of power is key for Tour de France contenders. Koen Pelgrim, a coach and physiologist at Deceuninck-Quick-Step, highlighted the importance of this aspect when he said: "The single most determinant of performance on a bike is your power to weight ratio. The power you put into the bike, resistance from riding uphill, and the balance between the two makes how fast you go uphill."

This number can change for riders depending on the length of the climb, with punchier climbers having much higher power to weight ratios on shorter ascents. But it isn't just elite riders who need to focus on their watts per kilo; amateur riders who

## CALCULATE YOUR POWER TO WEIGHT

| w/kg | 120w | 150w | 180w | 210w | 240w | 270w | 300w | 330w | 360w | 390w | 420w | 450w |
|------|------|------|------|------|------|------|------|------|------|------|------|------|
| 55kg | 2.2 | 2.7 | 3.3 | 3.8 | 4.4 | 4.9 | 5.4 | 6.0 | 6.5 | 7.1 | 7.6 | 8.2 |
| 60kg | 2.0 | 2.5 | 3.0 | 3.5 | 4.0 | 4.5 | 5.0 | 5.5 | 6.0 | 6.5 | 7.0 | 7.5 |
| 65kg | 1.8 | 2.3 | 2.8 | 3.2 | 3.7 | 4.1 | 4.6 | 5.0 | 5.5 | 6.0 | 6.5 | 6.9 |
| 70kg | 1.7 | 2.1 | 2.6 | 3.0 | 3.4 | 3.8 | 4.3 | 4.7 | 5.1 | 5.6 | 6.0 | 6.4 |
| 75kg | 1.6 | 2.0 | 2.4 | 2.8 | 3.2 | 3.6 | 3.0 | 4.4 | 4.8 | 5.2 | 5.6 | 6.0 |
| 80kg | 1.5 | 1.9 | 2.2 | 2.6 | 3.0 | 3.4 | 3.8 | 4.1 | 4.5 | 4.9 | 5.3 | 5.6 |
| 85kg | 1.4 | 1.8 | 2.1 | 2.5 | 2.8 | 3.2 | 3.5 | 3.9 | 4.2 | 4.6 | 4.9 | 5.3 |
| 90kg | 1.3 | 1.7 | 2.0 | 2.3 | 2.7 | 3.0 | 3.3 | 3.7 | 4.0 | 4.3 | 4.7 | 5.0 |
| 95kg | 1.2 | 1.6 | 1.9 | 2.2 | 2.5 | 2.8 | 3.2 | 3.5 | 3.8 | 4.1 | 4.4 | 4.7 |
| 100kg | 1.2 | 1.5 | 1.8 | 2.1 | 2.4 | 2.7 | 3.0 | 3.3 | 3.6 | 3.9 | 4.2 | 4.5 |
| 105kg | 1.1 | 1.4 | 1.7 | 2.0 | 2.3 | 2.6 | 2.9 | 3.1 | 3.4 | 3.7 | 4.0 | 4.3 |
| 110kg | 1.1 | 1.4 | 1.6 | 1.9 | 2.2 | 2.5 | 2.7 | 3.0 | 3.3 | 3.5 | 3.8 | 4.1 |

can improve this number will see a strong positive correlation in their performance. Despite the lower numbers compared to the pros, being able to increase it, even by a small amount, will lead to faster climbing times or easier ascents at the comparative power output.

The easiest but perhaps most expensive option for cyclists to improve their power to weight ratio is to shell out on a new bike, and instantly drop a few kilograms from their bike that they won't have to lug uphill. However, as much as we all want to mount a lightweight steed, it is more practical for our cycling performance and wallets to lose weight from our body rather than our bike in the long term. The weight you can also lose from dropping body weight greatly outweighs the savings on an upgraded bike. It may only be a few kilograms when upgrading your steed, but weight loss, over a well structured and sensible six-month training and nutrition plan, this number can be multiplied.

However it is important to realise the dangers of focusing on increasing your power to weight, as losing weight doesn't always mean you'll go faster uphill. Shedding useful muscle may in turn lower your power output, which may make you less efficient overall and a weaker rider in general for high-power efforts. Finding a balance is key to ensuring the weight you lose is going to be beneficial in the long run.

▼ Julian Alaphilippe has proved his ability over both short and steep ascents, as well as longer, more gradual climbs.

Training smarter not harder can prove invaluable come your big event day.

CHAPTER 12

# TRAINING TOOLS

To some, devising a training programme may appear quite daunting at first. The use of cycling-specific terminology, such as thresholds and training zones, along with the rise of power meters and heart-rate monitors can seem quite intimidating. But if you can utilise and understand these methods to their full potential, then you will start to train more smartly and see the benefits out on the road.

# TRAINING WITH POWER

▲ Ensuring your power meter is set up correctly before every ride is key for accurate and reliable results.

**The rise of the power-meter has been almost as pivotal to cycling as any previous technological development in the sport's history. Head back 25 years, and it would be rare to see a professional rider know what a watt is; nowadays they are commonplace amongst club riders and professionals know just how important they are to training. Their use in racing has even been criticised because, to some, it stagnates the spectacle of exciting and attacking riding.**

But when it comes to training with power-meters, they can be an extremely useful tool to fine tune your riding, but a lot of cyclists – with money to splurge – may purchase a power-meter for the sake of it and not really understand the numbers they produce.

There a number of ways power-meters can measure your power output, with the

strain gauge sitting on the pedal, the hub or the crank of the bike. All have varying benefits and costs, but if used consistently they will provide reliable and reusable results over time with each measuring the amount of power placed through the strain gauge for each pedal stroke.

Working with power-meters to benefit your training requires completing an FTP test (see pages 18–19), which calculates the maximum power you can sustain for 60 minutes. This test is vital initially, but it does need to be redone during your training programme to account for any improvements – or losses – in power output and plot them within your training plan accordingly.

This is another plus-point for power-meters as what is great about using and recording data over time is the ability to track your progress extremely accurately. Because the power output numbers aren't skewed by the terrain or weather, compared to heart-rate

▶ Discussing your power data with a coach can be a really constructive to get the most out of your ride.

measures, which can be affected by hydration, energy levels, muscle fatigue and temperature – all of which can subsequently skew training zones. But with instantaneous feedback a power-meter will always ensure you are training at the right levels.

As this immediate relaying of numbers comes through on your head unit, it may be wise to tweak your computer to provide average power-readings for the previous five seconds. This way you can get a better idea of what wattage you are riding at, rather than the sporadic and ever-changing numbers that initially show up.

▲ There are many different types of power meters, each with differing positive and negative aspects.

## TOP TIPS FOR POWER-METER TRAINING

Power-meters may seem fantastic, but there are a few key issues you should avoid when training with them:

• Forgetting to "zero offset" a power-meter before riding and then relying on inaccurate data can be problematic. Think of zero-offsetting a power-meter as the same process as resetting a set of measuring scales. Air pressure, ambient temperatures and other things can alter power-meter readings between rides. Therefore "zeroing" your power-meter before each ride clears the residual torque and sets an accurate baseline to work from.

• Confusing simple average power with normalised power; these are two entirely different readings. Normalised power accounts for intervals and efforts that have occurred over the entirety of the ride, but average power simply gives the average of the training session as a whole. This can lead to more intense sessions being misinterpreted when actually they were more fatiguing.

• Lastly, it is important to acknowledge the differences between indoor and outdoor riding. Indoor riding involves zero coasting and no air resistance – therefore is a more steady effort; outdoor riding can consist of many variables that can skew data, such as wind and drafting gains. Thus, comparing rides to each other can be an issue.

# TRAINING WITH HEART RATE

**The use of heart-rate monitors in recent years, thanks in part to the rise of the power-meter, has led to their use as being seen as a substandard method of analysing performance. Whereas power-meters do give instantaneous feedback to your power output, they are still a hefty investment to make. However, a heart-rate monitor can be bought relative cheaply, and it still gives a large swathe of data that can help you understand and manipulate your cycling training and performance.**

## DO'S AND DON'TS OF TRAINING WITH A HEART-RATE MONITOR:

• Use a combination of heart-rate monitors and power-meters if you have the option. Assessing power output and the consequences it has on your body, as well as implementing your own personal perception on the effort itself, is the pinnacle training tool.

• Don't exclusively rely on varying resting heart-rate values as a signal sign of illness. Studies have shown that although it is sometimes the case, isn't full proof.

• Don't expect your heart-rate to remain consistent across all types of conditions. A number of different factors such as altitude, ambient temperature and hydration status can all alter heart-rate values and their responses to training.

Heart-rate does have a slight delay to exercise intensity, however there is a benefit in that whereas a power-meter tells you how hard you are working physically, it doesn't tell you anything about how that stress is being perceived by the body. Similar to how a speedometer in a car will tell you how fast you are going, the rev meter will say what effect it is having on the car itself.

Riding to power-meters requires sticking to a set zone; it doesn't take into account external conditions, such as altitude, which will automatically raise heart-rate and lower your potential power-output compared to sea level.

Training with a heart-rate monitor requires accurately discovering your maximum heart-rate and plotting your training zones from there. You will find many methods which ask to enter your age, gender and fitness levels, and miraculously come up with a maximum heart-rate number. The old-school method of subtracting your age from 220 is also outdated, and whilst mildly accurate for generalising large swathes of the population, it isn't an ideal measure for an individual because there can be massive variations from one person to the next.

As a result, completing a 20–30 minute test is the ideal solution to find the correct number for you. There are many different protocols to this, but one of the more basic test procedures consists as follows.

Locate a climb of at least five minutes in duration, but begin with a solid 15-minute warm-up prior to the start of the test so you are loose and ready to exert yourself.

Complete some of this warm-up on your chosen climb, so you can get an idea of the ascent itself, as well as getting used to seated and standing efforts and the gear-ratios required for maximum effort.

Once warmed up, begin the ascent, increasing the intensity every 30 seconds until you are sprinting and can't maintain that pace any longer. Rest between each set by rolling back down to the starting point before repeating three more times. At the end of the fourth set, take a 10–15 minute cool-down by spinning out the legs to clear any lactic acid build-up. Once you have uploaded the heart-rate data, there should be a clear point in the all out efforts where your maximum heart-rate was reached.

Once you have discovered your maximum heart-rate you can use the training zones guide (*see* pages 128–129) to set the correct levels that you need to train at for each session.

◄ Even though power meters may have overtaken heart rate monitors as the supreme performance measure, it can still give vital data.

# TRAINING ZONES

Breaking down cycling training into simple numbers can be difficult when we are dwarfed by so much information in the modern training age. The use of training zones can be really helpful to simplify all the digits and create a far more structured training programme that you can apply to work best for you.

One of the best things about using training zones for your rides is that they can be applied to sessions almost anywhere, such as on the road itself, on the turbo-trainer, or rollers, or even on a stationary bike with a built-in heart-rate monitor or power-meter, such as a Wattbike. When out on the open road, the weather or terrain doesn't need to majorly affect your training session either, because you can just stick to riding to your zones, so average speed is almost irrelevant.

There are other training-zone calculations that can go into more detail but the five key zones listed in the training-zone table hit the main areas required to carry out a structured training plan. They not only relate to intensity but also should replicate how a rider feels on the bike and their perceived exertion, as well as the length of effort that a zone should be ridden in.

Each zone is listed from one to five, and rises in intensity each time, from recovery rides and warm-ups at zone one, to sustained efforts at zone three, to all-out sprints at zone five. These zones can then relate directly to the percentage of maximal heart rate or percentage of your functional threshold power-values – which you should

▲ What may be a zone two effort for one cyclist, may be a zone four for another.

| Zone | Effort | You can | It feels like you're | Use it for... | % Max HR | % FT Power |
|------|--------|---------|---------------------|---------------|----------|------------|
| 1 | Easy | Chat freely | Warming up | Warm-ups, cool-downs and recovery | 60–65% | 56–75% |
| 2 | Steady | Speak one sentence at a time | Riding along in the bunch on the flat | Long rides | 65–75% | 76–90% |
| 3 | Brisk | Speak a few words at a time | Breathing deeply and working hard | Long efforts of 10–20 minutes | 75–82% | 91–105% |
| 4 | Hard | Say only one word at a time | Really attacking (perhaps on a climb) | Efforts lasting 2–8 minutes | 82–89% | 106–120% |
| 5 | Very hard | Grunt and gasp | Sprinting | Efforts lasting less than 2 minutes | 89%–MHR | 121%+lower opposite arms and legs. |

know before you carry out a structured training programme.

One of the pitfalls of training zones is that they can prove problematic when riding with other cyclists, such as friends or team-mates; after all, hat may be a steady zone two effort for you may be a hard zone four effort for them. Structuring your training sessions so that you can ride them at your own levels or with people who are at the same zone is an ideal way to get around this issue.

But also ensuring breakfast soothes his riders' minds as well.

▼ Utilising your training zones to perfection can mean your riding becomes more enjoyable and beneficial.

Setting out a structured plan can help break down any fears of the challenge ahead.

**CHAPTER 13**

# TRAINING PROGRAMME

A training programme should be very specific to your personal needs, day-to-day life and ultimately the goal you want to achieve. Having an idea of some of the sessions you want to try, and having a basic, easy-to-follow training plan and the path towards your end goal are the best ways to help you achieve it.

# MIXED TRAINING WEEK

▶ Utilising indoor training when short on time is a useful alternative to training out on the road.

Designing a training plan specifically tailored to your goals could make all the difference come race day. Your season's big targets may seem a long way off, but before you know it you'll be on that start line of your big event of the season. It can creep up on you, so staying focused is vital and maintaining some structure and forethought in your training will help you make the most of your time on the bike. This means putting an effective training plan into action, ensuring you arrive at those target events in prime condition. Setting accurate intensity levels are crucial to getting results. It is also important to start steady and build the plan as you progress, don't be afraid to adapt it for injuries or illness or increase training loads if you feel you can manage more.

| WEEK 1 | Mon | Tue | Wed | Thur | Fri | Sat | Sun |
|---|---|---|---|---|---|---|---|
| Type | Rest day | Turbo trainer | Rest day | Interval session | Rest day | Weight session | Endurance ride |
| Hours | | 1 | | 1.5 | | 1 | 3 |
| Description | | Race attack imitation<br><br>Immediately after the warm-up, the two minute 'race attack' will begin. Ride as hard as you can for two to three minutes to simulate an attack in a race, before riding at a steady Zone 3 pace for three minutes.<br><br>Complete three reps of this five-minute set, then complete a 10 minute Zone 2 spin before repeating a further three five-minute sets.<br><br>Finish with a 10 minute cool-down. | | Sweetspot intervals<br><br>0-20' - Warm up rising to zone 3<br><br>20-30' - Zone 4 sweetspot<br><br>30-40' - Zone 2 recovery<br><br>40-50' - Zone 4 sweetspot<br><br>50-60' - Zone 2 recovery<br><br>60-70' - Zone 4 sweetspot<br><br>70-90' - Cool down lowering down to zone 1 | | Core and leg focus<br><br>4x8 repetitions - Back squat<br><br>3x60 secs - Plank<br><br>3x45 secs - side plank (each side)<br><br>4x8 repetitions - alternate arm and leg raises<br><br>4x8 repetitions - alternate leg lunges | Focus on maintaining a zone 1-3 effort for the duration of the ride.<br><br>Ensuring a decent warm up the day after a weight session.<br><br>All about time on the bike rather than specific efforts. |

## TRAINING PROGRAMME

# SPRINTING FOCUS

When training for a long endurance event, the implementation of sprinting into a training plan may seem counter-intuitive. However, this skill is not just useful for the end of races when attempting to be the first across the finish line; it is can also be transferable to jumping across to groups and can build power for short steep hills. Both of these skills can be crucial in long endurance rides.

| WEEK 1 | Mon | Tue | Wed | Thur | Fri | Sat | Sun |
|---|---|---|---|---|---|---|---|
| Type | Rest day | Sprint session | Rest day | Half-hill sprints | Rest day | Endurance ride | Recovery ride |
| Hours | 0 | 1 | 0 | 1 | 0 | 3½ | 1½ |
| Description | | It is important that the body is warmed up prior to attempting sprint efforts. When completing the 30-second sprints, use the first five seconds to raise the cadence before shifting up to harder gears. Finish off the session with four sets of sprints of ten seconds; these should be completed in the biggest gear you can maintain. | | Start off the session with a 20-minute warm-up that prepares your body for near maximal efforts. Complete your one-minute efforts on a variety of terrain that contain a flat road and a short climb. Start your sprint on a flat road that leads onto a steep hill, so that you split the effort over flat and climbing sections. It is also important not to overcook yourself on the flat sprint before the hill even begins. Timing this effort can be tricky, but persevere and reap the rewards. | | Despite a focus on sprinting for the week, ensuring your endurance base is still ticked off is crucial. Maintain a zone 2–3 effort for the duration of the ride. | Don't push yourself too hard and enjoy the ride. This is the perfect opportunity to ride with some friends to the cafe. |

Tuesday:

| Time | Zone |
|---|---|
| 0–15 | 1–3 |
| 15–15:30 | 5 |
| 15:30–20 | 3 |
| 20–20:30 | 5 |
| 20:30–25 | 3 |
| 25–25:30 | 5 |
| 25:30–30 | 2 |
| 30–30:10 | 5 |
| 30:10–35 | 3 |
| 35–35:10 | 5 |
| 35:10–40 | 3 |
| 40–40:10 | 5 |
| 40:10–45 | 3 |
| 45–45:10 | 5 |
| 45:10–60 | 1–2 |

Thursday:

| Time | Zone |
|---|---|
| 0–20 | 1–3 |
| 20–21 | 4–5 |
| 21–25 | 3 |
| 25–26 | 4–5 |
| 26–30 | 3 |
| 30–31 | 4–5 |
| 31–35 | 3 |
| 35–36 | 4–5 |
| 36–40 | 3 |
| 40–41 | 4–5 |
| 41–45 | 3 |
| 45–60 | 1–2 |

◄ You may be training for a long day in the saddle, but completing sprint intervals can be great for your overall performance.

### TRAINING PROGRAMME

# CADENCE FOCUS

▶ Mixing up you cadence with low and high efforts can be really beneficial on all terrain.

Cadence is an area of cycling which is often forgotten by many riders. However, riding at a variety of cadences, for different amounts of time, can be really beneficial

out on the road when you are faced with different riding conditions. These two sessions implement both high- and low-cadence efforts and test the body in different ways during each stint.

| WEEK 1 | Mon | Tue | Wed | Thur | Fri | Sat | Sun |
|---|---|---|---|---|---|---|---|
| Type | Rest day | Leg-speed intervals | Rest day | Split cadence session | Rest day | Rest day | Endurance ride |
| Hours | 0 | ½ | 0 | 1.5 | 0 | 0 | 2½ |
| Descr. | | This session maintains the physiological response in zones 1 to 3 while, at the same time, building up leg speed. Keep an eye on your heart-rate when doing this session and reduce the gear if your heart-rate is going too high. | | This session is a split workout, featuring low and high cadence efforts. Work your leg strength – with its low-cadence and high-torque efforts – with the higher-cadence, low-torque efforts, working on cardio-respiratory fitness. | | | Look at implementing a few threshold efforts into this 2½-hour ride, not only to mix up the ride structure, but also to see if you feel any benefit from the cadence work you have put in earlier in the week. |

The workout is made up of two 10-minute intervals, which increase in cadence every two minutes from 95, 100, 105, 110, and 95 RPM.

| Minutes | Cadence | Zone |
|---|---|---|
| 0–5 | 90 | 1 |
| 5–7 | 95 | 1–3 |
| 7–9 | 100 | 1–3 |
| 9–11 | 105 | 1–3 |
| 11–13 | 110 | 1–3 |
| 13–15 | 95 | 1–3 |
| 15–17:30 | 90 | 1 |
| 17:30–19.30 | 95 | 1–3 |
| 19:30–21:30 | 100 | 1–3 |
| 21:30–23:30 | 105 | 1–3 |
| 23:30– 25:30 | 110 | 1–3 |
| 25:30–27:30 | 95 | 1–3 |
| 27:30–33 | 90 | 1 |

| Minutes | Zone | Cadence |
|---|---|---|
| 0-15 | 1 | Self-selected |
| 15-45 | 2 | 95-100rpm |
| 45-55 | 1 | Self-selected |
| 55-75 | 3 | 60-75rpm |
| 75-90 | 1 | Self-selected |

# FTP TESTING WEEK

▶ Retesting your FTP throughout your training plan can help nail down and adapt your training zones accordingly.

It is key to implement fitness testing throughout your plan, not just at the beginning. This way you can see if you are making improvements, and ensure that the training zones you are riding at are accurate as you progress throughout the season. Making sure you complete your test when you are fresh, and can give it your all, is key. Therefore if you are feeling fatigued, or not at your best, postpone the test for another day.

| WEEK 1 | Mon | Tue | Wed | Thur | Fri | Sat | Sun |
|---|---|---|---|---|---|---|---|
| Type | Hill repeats | Upper body and core | Rest day | FTP test | Rest day | Rest day | Endurance ride |
| Hours | 1½ | 1 | | 1 | | | 3 |
| Description | These four-minute hill efforts should be tough but maintainable over the session. You should Ensure your fifth effort is just as strong as the first. In between these four-minute climbs descend down the hill and along a flat section of road to recover.<br><br>Time / Zone<br>0–15 / 1–3<br>15–19 / 4–5<br>19–23 / 2<br>23–27 / 4–5<br>27–31 / 2<br>31–35 / 4–5<br>35–39 / 2<br>39–43 / 4–5<br>43–47 / 2<br>47–51 / 4–5<br>51–55 / 2<br>55–70 / 1–2 | High plank<br>3 x 30 seconds<br>Pull-ups<br>3 x 8 (can be assisted if needed)<br>Side plank<br>3 x 30 seconds<br>Dead bug<br>3 x 16<br>Narrow grip push-up<br>3 x 16 | | FTP test<br><br>Time / Effort<br>0–10 / Gentle warm-up spin<br>10–25 / Three sets of one-minute fast cadence, one-minute easy, three-minute spin<br>25–30 / Five-minute all-out effort<br>30–40 / 10-minute recovery spin<br>40–60 / 20-minute all-out<br>*TESTING EFFORT*<br>60–70 / Cool down<br><br>Multiply your testing-effort average result by 0.95 to find your FTP. | | | Utilising the data you gained from your FTP test, try out a number of efforts at different zones to see how they feel in a real-world setting. |

# DROP-DOWN WEEK

Typically, during a long-term training plan, it is important to implement a drop-down week, where the body can recover from the intense work it has been putting in and gain the benefits from the training effect. This isn't a case of completely winding down the body, but it does give the opportunity for the body to try other physical activities – at a lower intensity – to try and refresh the mind whilst the body is also recovering. This may involve a spot of cross-training in the pool, or a gentle run to maintain cardio-vascular output and the body ticking over. These weeks would ideally placed at four-, six- or eight-week intervals, depending on the length of your overall training plan

◄ Take your drop down week as the opportunity to ride with others at a leisurely pace.

► Utilising cross training methods such as swimming or running are a great way of keeping your mind and body fresh.

| WEEK 1 | Mon | Tue | Wed | Thur | Fri | Sat | Sun |
|---|---|---|---|---|---|---|---|
| Type | Rest day | Cadence technique | Rest day | Swimming | Rest day | Rest day | Endurance ride |
| Hours | 0 | ½ | 0 | 1 | 0 | 0 | 2½ |
| Description | | Focus purely on cadence and not on the gear you are pushing. Generating leg speed can be an easy way to increase your speed on the bike in the long run.<br><br>Time  Cadence<br>0–5  80<br>5–10  90<br>10–15  80<br>15–20  100<br>20–25  80<br>25–30  110<br>30–35  80 | | This session will depend on your swimming ability. But focus on time in the pool, rather than the intensity or strokes you perform. Ensure you are properly warmed-up, and cool down before taking on the bulk of your session, with focuses on breathing and technique rather than speed and power. | | | With the aim of the week being to let the body recover, take this ride very steadily and not with any major efforts. It isn't often a cafe ride is encouraged as part of the longest ride of the week but this is the week to implement it. |

# TRAINING PROGRAMME
# ENDURANCE FOCUS

▶ Increasing your riding time on the bike is key to prepare yourself for your big event day.

Endurance weeks shouldn't be a case of heading out every day for five-hour rides. They will not only fry your mind but also won't be as effective a training tool as mixing in more intense endurance-based rides that are endurance-themed, but can be completed in a shorter time. The importance of the long weekend ride is still crucial to any training plan.

| WEEK 1 | Mon | Tue | Wed | Thur | Fri | Sat | Sun |
|---|---|---|---|---|---|---|---|
| Type | Rest day | Intense endurance ride | Rest day | Endurance and sprints | Rest day | Rest day | Endurance ride |
| Hours | 0 | 1 | 0 | 2 | 0 | 0 | 4½–5 |
| Description | | The goal of this session is to provide a training stimulus that can serve as a useful stand-in for endurance rides out on the road. It is also very useful for when the weather turns and riding may be treacherous, or when time is short and you need to complete a shorter session.<br><br>Minutes   Zone<br><br>0–5     1–2<br><br>*5–9   2–3<br><br>*9–10  4–5<br><br>*Repeat five–minute block 10 times<br><br>55–60  1–2 | | Getting out after work or early in morning, when the days become longer, are the perfect times to up your mileage on the bike. After a steady warm-up, begin the first of three 20-minute sets. These are split up into a 15-minute zone 3 effort and a five-minute zone 4 effort. It is important that there is a clear definition between each interval. The second part of the ride consists of one-minute sprints which are complimented with four-minute rest periods, and make sure you give yourself time to complete a 20-minute cool down.<br><br>Time    Zone<br><br>0–20    1–2<br>20–35   3<br>35–40   4<br>40–55   3<br>55–60   4<br>60–75   3<br>75–80   4<br>80–85   2<br>85–86   5<br>86–90   3<br>90–91   5<br>91–95   3<br>95–96   5<br>96–100  3<br>100–120 1–2 | | | This ride is all about time on the bike and getting used to eating and drinking on the go during a long stint in the saddle. Ensuring your nutrition strategy is on point during long rides is key preparation for your big event day. |

# PEAK PERFORMANCE

▼ Testing yourself on local climbs is key to replicating the mountains of mainland Europe.

A month out from your event you should be looking at being at the top of your game, from a physical, psychological and skills point of view. The hard work that you have put in should all lead to you giving once last push in the final big training week before you begin to taper, ensuring that all physical areas of training have been covered in the lead up to the big day.

| WEEK 1 | Mon | Tue | Wed | Thur | Fri | Sat | Sun |
|---|---|---|---|---|---|---|---|
| Type | Rest day | VO2 max efforts | Rest day | Tempo cadence pyramid | Rest day | Rest day | Endurance ride |
| Hours | 0 | ½ | 0 | 1hr 20 minutes | 0 | 0 | 6 |
| Description | | This session aims to complete several efforts around your VO2 max, alongside recovery periods at a mixture of 1:1 and 1:2 ratios. | | In this session, try to keep the power within zone 3; don't be tempted to go harder to add variation to pace. The cadence pyramid is designed to replicate changes in cadence as well as build sustainable power. | | | Try to incorporate a full variety of terrain into this long steady zone 2–3 ride similar to that you may experience on your event day. Practice psychological strategies you may have picked up over your weeks of training to get through long rides and as always eat and hydrate to the conditions out on the road. |

Tuesday – VO2 max efforts:

| Minutes | Zone |
|---|---|
| 0–5 | 1–2 |
| 5–10 | 3 |
| 10–15 | 1–2 |
| 15–18 | 4 |
| 18–21 | 1–2 |
| 21–24 | 4 |
| 24–27 | 1–2 |
| 27–30 | 4 |
| 30–33 | 1–2 |
| 33–36 | 4 |
| 36–39 | 1–2 |
| 39–42 | 4 |
| 42–45 | 1–2 |
| 45–48 | 4 |
| 48–58 | 1–2 |
| 58–60 | 3–4 |
| 60–64 | 1–2 |
| 64–66 | 3–4 |
| 66–70 | 1–2 |
| 70–72 | 3–4 |
| 72–76 | 1–2 |
| 76–78 | 3–4 |
| 78–90 | 1–2 |

Thursday – Tempo cadence pyramid:

Start this session with a 30-minute zone 2 effort, interspersed with four 10-second maximal sprints. Follow this with a consistent zone 3 effort for the remainder of the session which is dictated purely by a cadence pyramid of five-minute intervals.

| Minutes | Zone | Cadence |
|---|---|---|
| *0–30 | 2 | |
| 30–35 | 3 | 90 |
| 35–40 | 3 | 80 |
| 40–45 | 3 | 70 |
| 45–50 | 3 | 60 |
| 50–55 | 3 | 70 |
| 55–60 | 3 | 80 |
| 60–65 | 3 | 90 |
| 65–70 | 3 | 100 |
| 70–80 | 2 | Cool down |

*Include four 10-second maximal sprints within the 30-minute effort

# EVENT WEEK TAPER

▶ Shaking you legs out and staying loose in the days before the event will be key ahead of your big ride day.

Ideally you should look to taper down for a full two weeks before your big event, so that when you arrive at your sportive or *Grand Fondo* you feel fresh and ready to ride. This doesn't mean taking a whole week off prior to a big day on the bike, as you are likely to feel sluggish when you start riding. Therefore, keep the body ticking over, but accounting for travel to the event can be a big hurdle in itself. Getting set up with your bike and ironing out any kinks that may have occurred during travel will mean that you feel relaxed ahead of the big day. With all the hard yards you have put in throughout the year, as you cross the start line now is the time to reap the rewards.

| WEEK 1 | Mon | Tues | Wed | Thurs | Fri | Sat | Sun |
|---|---|---|---|---|---|---|---|
| Type | Interval | Rest day | Endurance ride | Rest/ Travel day | Activation ride | EVENT DAY | Rest day |
| Hours | 1 | 0 | 2½ | 0 | 1½ | 6 As fast as you want… | 0 |
| Description | Concentrate on shorter intervals but not at a maximal intensity to keep the body awake to intense efforts.<br><br>0–20' – warm up<br>20–22' – Zone 4<br>22–25 – Zone 2<br>25–27— Zone 4<br>27–30 – Zone 2<br>30–35 – Zone 2<br>35–37— Zone 4<br>37–40 – Zone 2<br>40–42— Zone 4<br>42–45 – Zone 2<br>45–60' – Cool down | | Focus on maintaining a steady zone 1–3 effort, just to keep the body ticking over ahead of the weekend. | | Focus on getting the body loose after sitting on a plane or car for a prolonged time your legs, lower back and hips will be craving a gentle spin ahead of the big day. | You've done all you can with your training, just relax and enjoy the day. | |

Being psychologically strong on the climbs and descents can be key to overcoming these huge challenges.

# CHAPTER 14

# PSYCHOLOGY

Training your body for the bike is just one step to reaching your full potential. Training your mind is another crucial process if you want to achieve the sometimes seemingly impossible: to conquer the climbs, demolish the descents and master riding massive days in the mountains with ease. Therefore, tapping into the psychological demands cycling can bring, and the mechanisms to overcome them, are things every rider should explore.

# ACHIEVING THE INCREDIBLE

▲ Ensuring you are psychologically strong can be key to conquering mammoth physical challenges.

**Psychology plays a huge role within all sports, and cycling is no different when the challenge of multiple mountains and hundreds of kilometres of road lie ahead. It is not just your physical fitness, how well you fuel your body, and the weather conditions on the day that can affect your performance. You won't be able to perform at your best if your mental state isn't at its peak. Finding a method that controls and channels nervous energy into a positive attitude will lead to a greater performance out on the road.**

Despite the romance that seems to be a constant overtone to the so called "mythical" climbs that are ridden during Grand Tours, every cyclist at any level will approach these climbs differently. Some will thrive in the amphitheatre of the iconic mountains, whereas other will shy away and fear the monstrous ascents that dwarf all those around them.

However, there are many ways you can break down these routes into somewhat unromantic and basic numbers. Each climb can be reduced to manageable and slightly less glamorous line graphs, showing the elevation, distance and gradient. In today's world, the data and content available on what were previously far-flung remote mountaintops, is no

## PREPARING FOR THE WORST

It may be seenm on the surface, as adopting a negative attitude before your big event day, but being realistic with the challenges that lie ahead, along with any other worries and fears, and then analysing them may make you far more confident when you line up on the start. Thinking rationally in the months before the event – rather than when they happen during it – can help cure any anxieties. Your "what if..." planning may be based around descending with other riders who have honed their craft over the years, or being stranded at the side of the road with a mechanical issue and limited knowledge of how to get going again. If you are honest with yourself, facing worst-case scenarios – such as practicing your descending or basic mechanical expertise – and not ignoring them, will mean that if they unfortunately come up on the big day, you won't panic and be able to get on with the situation at hand. This will leave your mind clearer and able to focus on the task of completing the ride ahead.

longer as hard to find. And now, a plethora of peaks have video footage of the roads to the summit, where cyclists can imagine themselves on the climb itself.

A key psychological tactic before you arrive at the climb itself may be to get a feeling of what the climb looks like. You can visualise the challenge before you even arrive at the destination, sense what the temperatures may feel like and view certain checkpoints to mark along the route. This imaging of climbs, descents and roads in between will make the event seem more realistic and trick the brain into thinking you have already done it.

This confidence of believing that you've sussed out the climb, knowing what to expect and realising the tricky aspects of the road you may have to take easy are key coping mechanisms when you line up at the bottom. If you know how you are going to tackle and get through a climb because, in your head, you have lived through it already makes it much easier when you get there.

It may not be possible to put a percentage on the amount psychology plays in performance, but without a strong mental mindset, the possibility of riding to your peak performance isn't possible.

▼ Major mishaps can even happen to the best riders in the world, such as Chris Froome on Mont Ventoux in 2016.

# CONQUERING THE CLIMBS

Completing mammoth rides are typically highlighted by cresting colossal mountains along the way. There is no greater challenge than scaling these ascents on two wheels. The psychological obstacle of seeing the climb itself brings the knowledge of knowing what lies ahead. For some, this may be the physical pain of the effort itself; for others, it may be the realisation that they are about to get dropped by their ride partners. These climbs are where Grand Tours are won and lost, and one of the main reasons why novices start riding a bike in the first place.

Sports psychologist Dr Josephine Perry believes in a term called "chunking" when it comes to breaking down the physical and mental challenge of riding a lengthy ascent, "Breaking down the whole ride or

▲ Visualising the climb with the use of videos, photos or maps can be a useful tool before you ride the climb itself.

## MENTALLY PREPARING FOR THE CLIMB AHEAD

- Focus on one climb at a time. If you are on a long ride with multiple climbs, don't worry about the challenges that lie ahead; just focus on the one that faces you next. Use the same technique as breaking up the climb, but break up your ride into sections.

- Pacing your ride may be seen as purely physical, but making sure that your mind keeps your speed and exertion under control is crucial so that you don't bonk before the summit.

- Looking up towards the top of the climb can distort your mind with how far you have to go. However, looking slightly ahead at the ground in front of the wheel can trick your mind that you are riding along on a far less steep gradient.

- Being mentally strong and being overconfident are different things. You should realise what your body is saying to you, as climbing can be extremely tough going, but there is a difference between not giving in and pushing your body to a level from which you are unable to recover.

- Riding the same climb over and over again in training may become extremely monotonous, but being able to ride up a climb in all sorts of conditions and physical states will make it seem a lot less daunting.

the whole climb into chunks makes it feel much more manageable" she said. "We really want to break down the big scary thing into lots more smaller things."

She explains how this can be done with any ride or climb: "The Alpe d'Huez has its switchbacks, which is a really nice and easy way to break it into chunks. Other ways are with certain villages you might go through. Having little bits on your climb to be able to chunk it down. When you are focused it is not about 'I've got to get to the top', it's 'I've got to get to that switchback, then I can refocus.' How you do that will be highly dependent on the ride or climb that you are doing, but videos can be brilliant for giving you landmarks to build into that."

Using psychology as an extra tool to your training can be a useful weapon, and one that Perry thinks most cyclists can use to their benefit, especially when climbing. "The beauty of psychology is you can use it to prepare for the stuff that scares you, which often is the big climbs. The biggest way to build up confidence is, firstly, to be really well prepared and, secondly, to have done things lots of times before. The first time you do a big climb it may be terrifying, the second and third times it may be scary, because you know what is coming, but you feel better because you know you have made it up before. What we want to do in training is to practice as close to the real thing as possible. Box Hill in Surrey is never going to give you the equivalent of Alpe d'Huez but if you do hill reps up Box Hill regularly, it will help you start to feel confident and more prepared for what you are about to do."

▼ Setting checkpoints in your mind, such as the next hairpin or road sign can be useful psychological markers.

# DARING DESCENTS

**The feeling of descending from the summit of a mountain at high speed can bring a mixture of wary feelings and internal worries for cyclists. The fear of descending isn't something that can be controlled easily. It should be honed over time, and revisited after setbacks, instead of forcing a "no-fear" approach to the situation throughout each descent you make.**

▲ It isn't just amateurs who can have issues with descending, Thibaut Pinot and Sir Bradley Wiggins have both had hiccups going downhill in their careers.

What makes descending skills a tricky psychological proposition is that the speed at which you are descending is probably as fast and safe as you are willing to go. Therefore, the need to go faster isn't exactly appealing, as Dr Josephine Perry, a member of the British Psychological Society, explains:

"Nobody is born knowing how to descend, and the people who just go off and do it are usually the people who are going to get injured. So, just as you learn any other skill, see this one as just that, and break it down into, 'How do I do this safely and effectively', and that will give you confidence."

Sports psychologists use two theories to combat these fears: first is a cognitive behavioural approach which breaks down skills into tiny steps. Through education on the skill itself, and completing repetitive training and increasing the difficulty: this may be: completing a short downhill; then a longer one; next a downhill on a bendy road; and finally on one covered with fallen leaves.

Perry explains the other approach,

which is Acceptance and Commitment Therapy (ACT): "ACT is where you look at your rational fears, such as going down a mountain very fast, but also looking at your values and what matters most to you. For some, the time wouldn't matter over the enjoyment and experience, so they are not going to push themselves to descend very fast as it destroys their experience. For somebody who is focused on the time, or wanting a certain medal out of it, then their value is about pushing themselves as fast as they can, and being the best that they can be. This might well override that fear."

Even on the occasions where riders want to go fast and have that as a pure goal, descending still has a major psychological element that can override it if you have a mishap. This has been shown with a number of pro riders, including stars of the sport, such as Thibaut Pinot and Bradley Wiggins, who have suffered from psychological lapses on descents, which have lost them stages or races. Even though they may have completed hundreds of miles of descents in practice, it is still a skill that can desert them from time to time, and this can happen to amateurs just as easily.

As Dr Perry said: "You get some people who are overconfident with descending, go with a kamikaze style down a mountain and put themselves – and other people – in danger. Absolutely, you want to be confident, but the key word is trust, you've got to trust yourself, and the way to do that is by doing something loads of times effectively and not getting hurt."

Establishing this trust, can be done in a number of ways: watching confident descenders, and which lines they take, and the speed at which they take corners, can help slowly build up confidence.

▼ Visualising the descent in your head and assessing your goals will lead to safe descending.

The mountains of the Tour de France are some of the most stunning natural amphitheatres in sport.

CHAPTER 15

# CLIMBS OF THE TOUR

When you think of the Tour de France, the images from the gruelling mountain stages are what makes the race and the iconic pictures create memories that last a lifetime. However, each ascent has its own individual story and unique characteristics, it almost gives the climb its own personality as amateur cyclists tame the climbs that the pros try to conquer each and every year.

# RIDING IN THE PYRENEES

▲ Fans from all countries and allegiances flock to the Pyrenees year in, year out.

**Despite often being overshadowed by the Alps as a preferable cycling holiday destination, a trip to the Pyrenees will never disappoint. Arguably, it is a more attractive port of call for a cyclist than its mountain-range cousin, not only because there is an abundance of cycling infrastructure in place but also the way the Pyrenees' climbs are stacked upon each other, making them perfect for long, looped rides out on the road.**

When there are more than 500 climbs in the Pyrenees with peaks over 1,000 metres elevation you are almost spoilt for choice. Whereas the Alps have longer climbs, the valley roads that need to be negotiated in between these ascents can prove tricky to negotiate into rideable loops – especially for beginners. The Pyrenees are far more user-friendly when it comes to route-planning for all skills levels.

Another plus compared to the Alps is the distinctly smaller population. With

Toulouse the only major city nearby, there is little need for flow-through traffic on many of the local roads and especially the mountain passes which can ruin the ambience for cyclists.

Vélo Le Closier, based in La Barthe-de-Neste, provides accommodation suited for cyclists, as well as a delicious breakfast and dinner to refuel after a long day out on the bike. They also offer guidance and advice on the best routes to cover in the area, including a variety of Tour de France icons, such as the Col d'Aspin and Col du Tourmalet, and ones not featured, such as Lac de Cap-de-Long.

Other towns that are ideal for cyclists to set up base are Luz-Saint-Sauveur, the starting point of the western side of the Col du Tourmalet and Luz-Ardiden, and Argèles-Gazost, which is ideally placed for the Hautacam and Eastern side of the Col d'Aubisque. The options available in the Pyrenees are vast and varied, and that is before you have even covered the options available in Spain and Andorra over the same mountain range.

◄ There are an abundance of climbs within the Pyrenees for amateurs to take on, from Grand Tour goliaths to rarely ridden gems.

▶ Steve Cummings outsmarted home favourites Thibaut Pinot and Romain Bardet in 2015 on the finish to Mende.

# PYRENEAN TRAVEL GUIDE

**HOW TO GET THERE:** Toulouse is the nearest major airport with regular daily flights from all over Europe. Other local airports, such as Carcassonne, Perpignan, Tarbes, Pau and Biarritz, may provide alternative options, depending on the time of year and departing airport locations.

**LOCATION IN FRANCE:** South-west France

**CLIMATE:** Despite the Pyrenees being further South, and typically hotter and more humid than the rest of France, it is still subject to indifferent weather throughout the year. What may be 30-degree sunshine in the valley could easily be 0-degree and snowing at the summit of the Tourmalet.

**NEARBY CITIES:** Toulouse, Pau, Tarbes and Lourdes

**STEVE CUMMINGS, FORMER DIMENSION DATA RIDER AND TWO-TIME TOUR DE FRANCE STAGE-WINNER**

"If I'm honest I really like the Pyrenees, they have a special place in my heart. You get the Basque fans, which is pretty cool because they love cycling and some of the best cycling fans in the world. My favourite climb is the Col d'Aspin, for many reasons, not least because of my stage win in 2016, but the Aspin is also a little less steep, so you go a bit quicker. So when you are alone, there is this anticipation from the supporters who have waited there all day waiting for the first rider to come through. I remember crossing the top and just seeing Union Jack flags flying and I was trying to stay calm because I had to get down the descent.

"Another climb that always sticks out for me is Port de Balès, because it is brutal and I remember, when I was with BMC, I had a really bad crash which actually almost finished my Tour. I went back again when I was national champ and crested the climb first. The crowd is really in your face and when you are in front, you know everyone is watching. I wasn't thinking about it at the time because you are in your own little internal zone, not letting external factors bother you, but you know they are there.

"The climbs in the Pyrenees are similar to where I lived in Italy, less regular than the Alps and the gradients are that bit steeper. When I was in top shape they were more manageable, mainly because the Alps are just so long. Descending in the Pyrenees is a little slower as well as the roads are tighter and not as vast as the Alps."

The coloured bicycles and cattle are part of the landscape atop the Col d'Aubisque.

# CLIMBS OF THE TOUR
# LUZ-ARDIDEN
## FROM LUZ-SAINT SAUVEUR

LENGTH: **13.1KM**
AVERAGE GRADIENT:
**7.9%**
HEIGHT OF SUMMIT:
**1,715M**
TOTAL METRES
ASCENDED: **1,036M**

▲ Lance Armstrong and Iban Mayo crash in 2003 after getting tangled in a supporters bag.

**You may be forgiven for thinking Luz-Ardiden as a forgotten ascent compared to the mammoth Col du Tourmalet across the Pays Toy valley, but underestimate it at your peril. Think of it as a one-two punch, rather than an afterthought, as it is a must ride Pyrenean challenge, equal in terms of beauty and punishment.**

The climb rises out of Luz-Saint Sauveur on the D12, which is also the start town of the Western ascent of the Col du Tourmalet. Despite Luz-Ardiden being six kilometres shorter in length to the Col on the other side of the cycling town, it is by no means less of a challenge and the views at the top are equal to those on the Tourmalet.

Even though officially he has been written out of Tour de France history record books, Luz-Ardiden was the dramatic setting when Lance Armstrong was brought down by a spectator's bag catching in his handlebars. The tangle led to the American, and Iban Mayo, falling to the tarmac, as his main rival Jan Ullrich sportingly waiting up the road for leaders to reconsolidate. Armstrong lit the blue touchpaper upon catching his German rival and blasted his way to the top to take the stage win and later the overall title. This yellow jersey – along with his other six – was eventually taken away.

The climb has been used as a summit finish one other time, in 2011, when Spaniard Sammy Sánchez took the win to the delight of the Basque fans riding for Euskaltel-Euskadi, who invade the Pyrenean mountain stages year in, year out.

As Pyrenean ascents go, Luz-Ardiden has a gentle start of around 6% for the first few kilometres as you rise out of the town. The village of Grust, which signifies about nine kilometres to go, is where the steady gradient from the start kicks up for a couple of kilometres and is arguably the toughest section of the overall climb.

As the tree cover, which has been welcome shelter for the duration of the climb so far, fades away with four kilometres to go, the climb opens up to the elements but also glorious views, with the switchbacks snaking their way up the mountain above you. As you progress, the shoelace road

**Luz-Ardiden**
1 715 m - km 211 -
(13,3 km à 7,4%)
HC

736m Luz-Saint-Sauveur - **km 197,7**

830m Sazos - **km 199,5**

999m Grust - **km 201,5**

1 700m
1 600m
1 500m
1 400m
1 300m
1 200m
1 100m
1 000m
900m
800m
700m

300m at 6,8%

**KEY**
From 3 to 5,9 %
From 6 to 8,9 %
From 9 %

Average percentage per kilometer

5,5  6  8  8  10  8,5  8  8,5  9  6,5  7  6,8
1  2  3  4  5  6  7  8  9  10  11  12  13

draped out underneath you shows just how far you have risen in a short time.

There are a few sections where you may be diverted off the main route to the top, at four kilometres to Viscos on the D149, and at 1.5 kilometres to the summit, where it's important to stay left towards Aulian.

Alpe d'Huez may get all the attention with its 21 hairpin bends, but Luz-Ardiden has 25 of them and it is certainly up for debate as to which has the more picturesque road to the summit. Similar to its switchback sibling over in the Alps, Luz-Ardiden is a dead-end ski station. However, due to its far smaller stature, the road is very quiet in the summer months when the resort is shut down.

Its location, near to the Spanish border, has meant Luz-Ardiden has not only hosted Tour de France finishes but also Vuelta a España conclusions, the most recent being in 1995, when Laurent

Jalabert took the honours on his way to securing overall victory. Despite not having a through-road option for the pros to take in racing circumstances, it means you will have to descend on the same road you scaled to the summit, and it is just as enjoyable, with its straight flowing roads, incredible views and technical hairpins to challenge your cycling prowess.

▲ Watching the Tour requires advanced logistical planning if you are to find a spot on the climb.

▼ The Basque fans always come out in force when the Tour visits the Pyrenees.

# COL DU TOURMALET

## WESTERN APPROACH FROM LUZ-SAINT SAUVEUR

LENGTH: **19KM**
AVERAGE GRADIENT: **7.4%**
HEIGHT OF SUMMIT: **2,115M**
TOTAL METRES ASCENDED: **1,410M**

**The Col du Tourmalet and the Tour de France go hand in hand when it comes to cycling folklore. The most ascended climb in the race's history is based around its nickname, l'Incontournable – the unavoidable – as it is the only road through this section of the Pyrenees and is a key link to other climbs in the area. Despite its inevitability in the Tour almost every year, the Tourmalet is arguably one of the most iconic climbs in cycling, one adored by amateurs and professionals alike.**

There are two ways to the summit, and they have almost identical lengths and gradients, with the false flat that greets you at the beginning of the Eastern side

▲ The weather on the Tourmalet can be ever changing, from snow and rain one day to sweltering sun the next.

skewing the gradient further up the road. The western side may have hosted stage finishes and be more picturesque but, from the Eastern side, the story of Eugène Christophe and his broken forks is written in Tour de France folklore. The Frenchman had mechanical issues on the descent and walked down the Tourmalet to Saint-Marie de Campan, where he forged a new front fork from 22mm steel with the help of a seven-year-old boy working the bellows. Christophe suffered a 10-minute time penalty for taking outside assistance as he finished three hours and 50 minutes behind the stage-, and eventual Tour-winner, Philippe Thys.

The western side is a long 19-kilometre slog from Luz-Saint-Sauveur, with upwards of 1,410 vertical metres to the summit at 2,115m. These numbers need to be respected as it is key for cyclists to pace their ride, as it will be pivotal in maintaining a steady speed all the way to the high-altitude finish at the top.

This is perhaps most important when rolling out of Luz-Saint-Sauveur as the gradient is at its most forgiving, staying below 8% for the first six kilometres, before the first major settlement of Barèges. This village has plenty of shops and cafes to pop in to if you are taking a more leisurely ride to the summit, but also gives a slight respite in gradient – dropping to 5% – before kicking out of the village above 8% which is par for the course for the remainder of the ascent.

Just past Barèges, there is a small fork in the road towards the Voie Laurent Fignon

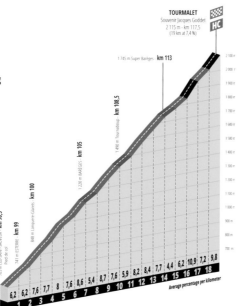

– named after the two-time winner of the Tour de France. This was the old road until it was washed away in the early 2010s. It has since been reconditioned and is now a one-way cycle-only path, which looks down on the valley and the new road which winds its way up to the ski station at Super Barèges. The last major checkpoint before the summit, is at 4.5 kilometres to go, with Le Bastan cafe the final opportunity to stock up on supplies before the last push towards the switchbacks that loom above the valley.

As these switchbacks twist and turn out of Super Barèges to face the summit once again, the sight of the cable car up to the Pic du Midi comes into view on a clear day. With four kilometres to go, the signs which have guided you up the ascent will give you the ominous warning that the percentages of the last few kilometres are set to ramp up into double figures.

This is where you will know if your pacing strategy has paid off, or if you let your fresher legs at the bottom of the climb get the better of you. As the final kilometre lays down the toughest section of the climb – grinding through the double-digit gradients – you are greeted with the sight of the iconic Octave Lapize statue. The Frenchman was the first rider to reach the top of the Col du Tourmalet in 1910 and this monument of him gasping for breath at the summit gives a strong resemblance to every cyclist that has followed him.

▼ From both the Western and Eastern ascent of the Tourmalet, the final kilometres of the climb are the steepest.

# CLIMBS OF THE TOUR
## COL D'AUBISQUE
### WESTERN APPROACH FROM LARUNS

LENGTH: **16.6KM**
AVERAGE GRADIENT:
**7.2%**
HEIGHT OF SUMMIT:
**1,709M**
TOTAL METRES
ASCENDED: **1,190M**

"Take the riders up the Aubisque? You're completely crazy in Paris." These are the words of the local road engineer who was asked by Alphonse Steinès – a colleague of Tour de France director Henri Desgrange – to clear the mountain pass to race the 1910 Tour de France. This devilish route, including the passing of the Col du Tourmalet on a brutal 326-kilometre slog from Luchon to Bayonnem has since been nicknamed "Circle of death". When stage-winner Octave Lapize saw Steinès, he raged at him: "Vous êtes des assassins! Oui, des assassins!" (You are murderers! Yes, murderers!). A number of riders finished a whole day behind Lapize.

▲ Stephen Roche took a memorable Irish 1-2 ahead of Sean Kelly on the Aubisque in 1985.

**KEY**

From 0 to 2,9 %
From 3 to 5,9 %
From 6 to 8,9 %
From 9 %

Col des Bordères
1 156 m - km 159,5
(8,6 km at 5,8%)

Col d'Aubisque
1 709 m - km 180,5 -
(16,6 km at 4,9%)

HC

Average percentage per kilometer

The Col d'Aubisque is a perennial feature of the Tour de France, often used via its many routes linking up with other Pyrenean beasts on mountain stages with regular stage finishes in Pau, 50 kilometres north of the Aubisque. It has, however, hosted three Tour de France finishes in 1971, 1985 and 2007. The second of these was a short and sharp shoot out on a split stage day, from Luz-Saint-Sauveur. At just 52.5 kilometres long stage winner Stephen Roche took a memorable Irish 1-2 beating out countryman Sean Kelly by 1:03, but it wasn't all plain sailing as Roche explained in his book 'Born to Ride'.

"There were lots of attacks, notably from Lucho Herrera, he went off early on the climb and got a decent gap. Then I made my move from the group behind, caught Herrera and went straight past him. Gem [Raphael Geminiani - Roche's Directeur Sportif] had been telling everyone for the last nine months that I was going to win this stage, so I couldn't let him down."

The stage win solidified his podium position behind the La Vie Clare duo of Greg Lemond and home favourite Bernard Hinault who would go on to win the Tour that year.

There are three ways to the top of the Aubisque: the Western ascent is the most common; the eastern ascent, via the Col du Soulor, can involve taking in descents and flat sections from Ferrieries and Argelès-Gazost; and the Soulor can also be ascended from Ferrières from the North.

The first few kilometres are sheltered and only touch around 4-5% in gradient,

so you should be able to maintain a decent cadence and rhythm up to Eaux-Bonnes. But as soon as you leave this town, the road ramps up and the shelter disappears as the climb begins to bite back. The steepest 13% section isn't long, but is important to be aware of. so you aren't caught out when it kicks up.

The climb hasn't just been used in the Tour de France. As recently as 2016, the Vuelta a Espana paid a visit on stage 14. Here Dutchman Robert Gesink took his first Grand Tour stage win on the Pyrenean peak, when he out sprinted and out witted Frenchman Kenny Elissonde and Russian Egor Silin in the final couple of kilometres.

The town of Gourette is the last settlement before the summit, at 12 kilometres so, if you need to fill any bottles or buy any supplies, this is the place to stock up. The hard work of grinding to the top is all worth it for the final three kilometres as the landscape opens up and you are treated to dwarfing mountains all around. The cafe at the summit is open year-round and you'll be keen to refuel next to the bust of Lucien Buysse who won the 1926 Tour de France, as well as the yellow, green and polka-dot bike statues which are stationed at the top of the climb.

There is a reason the Tour keeps coming back here, and once you have conquered the Col d'Aubisque you'll understand why.

▲ The Aubisque is one of the most picturesque ascents in the entire Pyrenees.

# COL D'ASPIN
## VIA THE EASTERN APPROACH FROM ARREAU

LENGTH: **12KM**
AVERAGE GRADIENT: **6.5%**
HEIGHT OF SUMMIT: **1,490M**
TOTAL METRES ASCENDED: **779M**

**It may be seen as a little brother to the Col du Tourmalet – it exceeds the Col d'Aspin in stature, length and average gradient – but the Aspin's role in the Tour de France has been well and truly cemented and is a must-ride for all cyclists heading the Pyrenees.**

It has been ascended more than 70 times in the Tour de France, in part due to its location, north of the Tourmalet, as well as being relatively close to other climbs, such as the Col de Peyresourde to the east. It makes the Col d'Aspin the perfect link climb for Tour de France stages from both its eastern and western approaches.

The western approach starts from Saint-Marie-de-Campan – the same as the eastern approach for the Col du Tourmalet – and averages a far gentler 5% gradient over its 12.8-kilometre ascent to the summit of the pass. The eastern road, which leaves from Arreau, is trickier and averages 6.5% on the D918.

Compared to other Grand Tour climbs, the Aspin is very narrow and gives an old-school feel despite its immaculate road surface. Without much traffic heading up or down the climb, it almost feels like a juiced-up cycle lane at times. In fact, it is more likely you will come across roaming cattle than the roar of a car engine as the road weaves and snakes it way up through farmer' fields, including an unconventional hairpin about three kilometres in that mimics that of a capital P.

You may often hear the Aspin described as "easy" compared to other climbs, but anyone who has ridden in the Pyrenees will tell you that word is rarely used when it comes to riding uphill in the region. Admittedly, the Aspin starts gently and never tips over 5% for the first few kilometres, with the steepest section hitting 9% around half way up. But the views back down towards Arreau and over the river Neste and the lush green mountains of the Pyrenees certainly keep you going straight from the beginning of the climb. Using the kilometer-markers at the side of the road will help gauge your effort, keeping you in the know for the distance to the top, elevation and the

▼ Julian Alaphilippe crested the Col d'Aspin first on his way to securing his King of the Mountains jersey in the 2018 Tour.

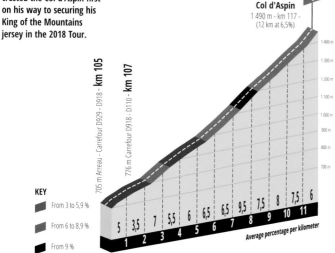

**Col d'Aspin** 1
1 490 m - km 117 -
(12 km at 6,5%)

705 m Arreau - Carrefour D929 - D918 - **km 105**

776 m Carrefour D918 - D110 - **km 107**

1 400 m
1 300 m
1 200 m
1 100 m
1 000 m
900 m
800 m
700 m

**KEY**
From 3 to 5,9 %
From 6 to 8,9 %
From 9 %

| 5 | 3,5 | 7 | 5,5 | 6 | 6,5 | 6,5 | 9,5 | 7,5 | 8 | 7,5 | 6 |
|---|---|---|---|---|---|---|---|---|---|---|---|
| 1 | 2 | 3 | 4 | 5 | 6 | 7 | 8 | 9 | 10 | 11 | |

*Average percentage per kilometer*

average percentage in gradient for the next kilometre of the climb.

Despite its serene and quiet nature nowadays, the 1950 edition of the Tour was far from it. As the Italian wearer of the maillot jaune, Fiorenzo Magni, and other race leaders, ascended the Aspin, angry spectators begun to boo and throw bottle caps at them. Another Italian, Gino Bartali, and Jean Robin, from France, both crashed, with Bartali even claiming a Frenchman came at him with a knife. Bartali insisted that both Italian teams, including Magni, should withdraw from the Tour and they duly obliged. Swiss

cyclist Ferdy Kübler took advantage to take the overall race win, but looking back at the decision Magni said: "I believe that there are bigger things than a technical result, even one as important as winning the Tour de France."

Towards the top of the climb, the last five kilometres average 8% as the road straightens out with slight bends and only the kilometer-signs as psychological markers to aim for. As you crest the summit of this Tour icon, you'll realise Tourmalet's little brother certainly packs a punch and holds its own amongst the Pyrenean greats.

▼ Geraint Thomas of Team Sky, Yellow Leader Jersey on Col D'aspin during the 105th Tour de France 2018.

# RIDING IN THE ALPS

▲ Fans always flock to the Alps to catch a glimpse of peloton rolling by.

▼ The scenery is always second to none in the Alps.

**It is no secret that the Alps are a cyclist's playground, with solid facilities for cyclists to stay and a plethora of climbs to cover, you won't be able to cover even a significant amount of them all in just one visit.**

Cycling tourism has increased in part thanks to the Tour de France. The smooth and regularly resurfaced roads are perfect for amateur cyclists to ride in the weeks, months and years after the pro peloton has moved on to the next Tour town, thanks to the frequent signs to local climbs, as well as kilometer-markers with elevation, gradient and distance-markers on the climbs themselves.

However, it is not just the behemoth mountains to have graced the Tour de France that can be the most attractive climbs for amateur cyclists. Hidden away off the classic routes seen on the Grand Tours are goat-tracks and single-lane roads that are in close proximity to their Tour de France icons. Their secluded state means they are unsuitable for motor vehicles, but are still challenging enough to match the stunning scenery in which they reside.

So where is best to set up base in the Alps? Luckily there are a number of options for you to base yourself.

The Maurienne Valley sits within striking distance of a number of brutish climbs, such as the Col de Madeleine, Col de la Croix de Fer and Col d'Iseran, as well as smaller but no less significant modern Tour icons such as Montvernier, which is a mini version of Alpe d'Huez.

Basing yourself in Bourg d'Oisans gives you the opportunity to ride the full-size Alpe d'Huez itself, but you are not far away from other beautiful climbs, such as Col de Sarenne, Col du Sabot and Col du Glandon from the South side – which is part of the infamous annual one-day cyclosportive for amateur riders La Marmotte Granfondo.

Another hotspot riding location is Briançon, which gives riders the opportunity to ride the Col d'Izoard and Col du Granon, as well as the Col du Galibier via the Col du Lautaret. For those who are feeling particularly strong, Italy and a host of other climbs aren't far away either.

## GERAINT THOMAS – 2018 TOUR DE FRANCE WINNER AND STAGE-WINNER ATOP ALPE D'HUEZ AND LA ROSIÈRE

"I think, when comparing the Alps to other climbs, the roads are a lot bigger and straighter, and a lot draggier and wider. They don't seem to be as harsh as the Pyrenees either, which can be twisty and steep and a bit of a rougher surface too.

"The Alps are just what you think of when you think of the Tour, with so many iconic climbs, and you always think of those mountain days that symbolise the whole race for me.

"Winning at La Rosière was the first every road stage that I won at the Tour de France which was obviously amazing, and then to back it up the next day with Alpe d'Huez, which is such an iconic climb. I remember watching stages from years ago – when Giuseppe Guerini crashed up there after a fan, with a camera taking a photo in the middle of the road, knocked him off his bike

– and all the stages going up there in the past. So the fact that I've won up there is just mad really. That was an amazing feeling and to win it with the yellow jersey was just incredible.

"My name on the sign was down as Thomas Geraint for a bit, but they have since rectified it, which is kind of the story of my life really, but you would think they would know by now. But I definitely want to go skiing when I finish racing and pay that a visit to show my boy as well."

▲ Geraint Thomas took his second stage win in as many Alpine days atop of Alpe d'Huez.

## ALPS TRAVEL GUIDE

**HOW TO GET THERE:** Grenoble is the closest airport to the Alps, but sometimes doesn't have great availability from the UK in summer months. Geneva and Lyon are ideal alternatives but are two-hour drives away.

**LOCATION IN FRANCE:** South-east

**CLIMATE:** Most climbs open towards the end of May and close after the end of September, but this does depend on the weather or snowfall that season, and the height of the climb in question.

**NEARBY CITIES:** Grenoble, Lyon, Geneva

Switchbacks and snowcapped mountains are typically on the menu when the Tour rolls into the Alps..

LENGTH: **30.5KM**
AVERAGE GRADIENT: **4.8%**
HEIGHT OF SUMMIT: **2,360M**
TOTAL METRES ASCENDED: **1,350M**

**When a climb has been at the epicentre of not one but two Grand Tours, you know it is something pretty special. The Col d'Izoard has history in both the Tour de France and has also played a significant role in the Giro d'Italia.**

Often used with finishes in the town of Briançon, on the northern side of the mountain, however, in 2017 the Izoard was the highest finish-point of that year's Tour de France. On stage 18, home rider Warren Barguil took the win wearing the polka-dot jersey ahead of the GC contenders, including eventual Tour-winner Chris Froome. Earlier in the day, Dutchwoman Annemiek van Vleuten rode away from the field with five kilometres to go to take the honours in La Course.

The first half of the southern side of the Izoard, from Guillestre, has a gentle run-in, rarely touching 5% gradient along the canyon road alongside the River Guil dipping in and out on tunnels carved through the rock. However, it is important not to get carried away as at more than 30 kilometres in length, the Izoard is one of the longest climbs in the Alps. In addition although the average gradient is 4.8%, it is a far more punishing 7.3% for the final 14 kilometres.

This harder second half starts with a left turn onto the D902 and the gradient kicks up immediately, before a long straight comes into view and the villages of Arvieux, La Chalp and Brunissard are passed with 10 kilometres to go. The straightness of the road can deceive you, as it seems you aren't gaining altitude and feels a lot tougher than it looks as you chug your way up the false flat road toward the imposing hairpins that lie ahead.

Despite the dense wooded hairpins, every now and then a gap in the trees will open up with stunning views down the valley, showing just how quickly the harsh gradients send you up the mountain. These views become more panoramic as you hit each hairpin which arrive with constant regularity.

Despite the abundance of trees surrounding the road, a feeling of suffocation can begin as the air becomes thinner as you approach 2,000 metres

▲ **Annemiek van Vleuten took race honours on the Izoard in the 2017 edition of La Course.**

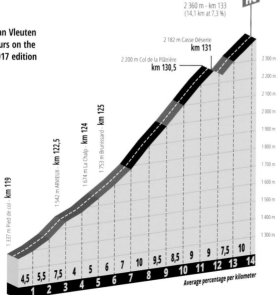

Col d'Izoard
2 360 m - km 133
(14,1 km at 7,3 %)
**HC**

2 182 m Casse Déserte
**km 131**

2 200 m Col de la Plâtrière
**km 130,5**

1 753 m Brunissard - km 125

1 674 m La Chalp - km 124

1 542 m ARVIEUX - km 122,5

1 337 m Pied de col - km 119

**KEY**
From 3 to 5,9 %
From 6 to 8,9 %
From 9 %

*Average percentage per kilometre*

elevation. However, it is the sight of the Casse Deserte at the top of this section that will truly take your breath away.

The arrival at the top of the hairpins and entrance into the rock-formed wonder also coincides with a flowing 500-metre descent before the final push to the top. The show-stopping vista is truly unique, with shark-tooth rocks jagging up from the cliff edge, make this a stunning location for the final four kilometres of the climb. These rocks are the backdrop to the plaque monuments within the rocks, recalling Louison Bobet and Fausto Coppi, who duked it out on this famous col back in the 1950s.

Make sure that you take advantage of the downhill, but stay wary of your gearing as the ramp kicks up quickly and timing the shift from the big to the small ring for the last section is crucial so you don't come to a standstill.

The final kick to the line is brutal and beautiful in equal amounts, touching close to 10% gradient as the switchbacks show a stunning view back down to where you have ridden. All this comes before the grand final corner which appears over the horizon as you join the pantheon of greats to summit the Izoard.

▼ The Casse Déserte will take your breath away, as well as signifying a few kilometres to the summit.

# COL DU GALIBIER
## NORTHERN APPROACH VIA COL DU TÉLÉGRAPHE

LENGTH: **34.5KM**
AVERAGE GRADIENT:
**5.5%**
HEIGHT OF SUMMIT:
**2,642M**
TOTAL METRES
ASCENDED: **2,089M**

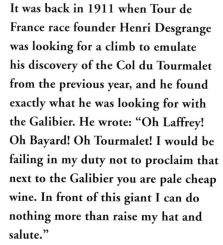

It was back in 1911 when Tour de France race founder Henri Desgrange was looking for a climb to emulate his discovery of the Col du Tourmalet from the previous year, and he found exactly what he was looking for with the Galibier. He wrote: "Oh Laffrey! Oh Bayard! Oh Tourmalet! I would be failing in my duty not to proclaim that next to the Galibier you are pale cheap wine. In front of this giant I can do nothing more than raise my hat and salute."

In its first appearance in the race, only three riders made it up to the top without walking. Probably to Desgrange's joy that he found a climb so tough it pushed the human limits.

One of the characteristics that makes the Galibier even more of an epic challenge is that both the northern and southern sides require riders to crest a separate Col before continuing to the summit of the Galibier.

The South side of the climb requires taking on the Col du Lautauret before the summit – there is a monument to Desgrange on this side of the ascent – but the northern side is better known and requires tackling the Col du Télégraphe before the main course of the Galibier.

The Télégraphe side is the more notorious and frequently-raced ascent out of the two and is arguably one of the toughest back-to-back assaults the sport has to offer. Rising to 1570 metres, the Télégraphe is a hefty climb in its own right. Scrambling its way up the mountain at a steady 7% for 12 kilometres from Saint-Michel-de-Maurienne, which, from above, looks like the road has been mapped out by a child trying to draw a straight line whilst driving a bumper car.

The short descent into Valloire knocks off 140 vertical metres and always seems slightly demoralising, rather than enjoyable, as there is no way in or out of this ski town without climbing once again. However tempting it may be to fly through and onto the Galibier, be wary, there is not much civilisation from here onwards so any supplies or recovery breaks should be taken here.

In the 2011 Tour, to celebrate the

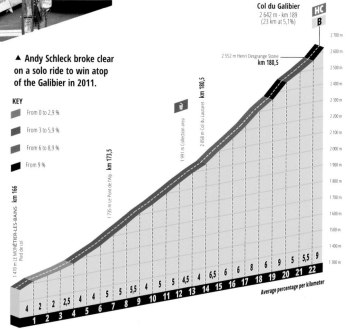

▲ Andy Schleck broke clear on a solo ride to win atop of the Galibier in 2011.

KEY
From 0 to 2,9 %
From 3 to 5,9 %
From 6 to 8,9 %
From 9 %

Col du Galibier
2 642 m - km 189
(23 km at 5,1%)

2 552 m Henri Desgrange Stone
km 180,5

2 058 m Col du Lautaret km 180,5

1 991 m Collection area

1 735 m Le Pont de l'Alp km 173,5

1 470 m LE MONÊTIER-LES-BAINS km 166
Pied de col

Average percentage per kilometre

100th anniversary of its first appearance, the Galibier was climbed twice, including a summit finish on stage 18 which was won by Andy Schleck – from the southern approach via the Lautauret. The peloton crested the ascent from the northern side the following day as home favourite Tommy Voeckler gallantly conceded the yellow jersey he had fought so hard to retain through the mountains to Schleck – though Cadel Evans would win won the GC.

The first few kilometres of the Galibier may seem gentle, as the straight road carves its way through sweeping slopes either side. However, it is important not to get carried away with the seemingly flat terrain as the climb gets tougher and tougher as the road slowly rises.

With eight kilometres to go, the road that has drifted through and above the valley takes a swinging right turn at Plan Lachat, which is usually greeted with a headwind and the beginning of the final steep section of the climb. Holding close to a 9% gradient from here to the top of the climb, it still seems to be a lifetime away as the road ascends skywards above you.

There might be a temptation, with one kilometre to go, to dip into the tunnel that takes you through to the other side of the climb, but if the summit is on your mind you must conquer the steepest, final kilometre ascent.

Reaching the summit of the Galibier feels almost out of this world. What may be high for amateurs is the same for the professionals as the "Souvenir Henri Desgrange" is awarded to the first rider to crest the highest point of that year's Tour de France. Given the Galibier's height of 2,642 metres it is quite often this summit when included in that year's parcours.

▼ The summit of the Galibier seems like another world away at 2,645 metres above sea level.

# ALPE D'HUEZ
## APPROACH FROM BOURG D'OISANS'

LENGTH: **13.8KM**
AVERAGE GRADIENT:
**8.1%**
HEIGHT OF SUMMIT:
**1,850M**
TOTAL METRES
ASCENDED: **1,124M**

▲ **Turn seven turns into a sea of orange as Dutch Corner becomes the epicentre of The Alpe when the Tour is in town.**

**Ask a non-cycling fan to name a famous climb of cycling, and the chances are Alpe d'Huez will be near the top of their list. This cycling Mecca is one ascent all cyclists must tick off their bucket list. It may not be the highest, hardest or longest climb in Tour de France history, but the 21 bends of Alpe d'Huez are a must-ride climb for amateurs and pros alike.**

Rising out of the town of Bourg d'Oisans, that sits in the Romanche Valley, the D211 climb hits you hard straight from the off with the first few straights being the biggest mental hurdles of the entire ascent. After what seems like a long slog up to bend 21 – they count down in reverse order to

the summit – another stretch of road that is more than 10% gradient once again comes into view. This harsh start thankfully eases upon reaching the first settlement on the climb of La Garde after two kilometres.

Each of the 21 bends is named after a former winner of the Tour de France stage, which not only gives a unique touch to the climb but also gives a psychological boost as you can tick off each individual hairpin bend on your way to the summit.

After long slogs of the first few steep stretches of road, bends 13 to 8 come in rapid succession, forming the picture-perfect sight over which fans reminisce when watching historic editions of the Tour de France on this famous Alp. Each of these hairpins also give you two options when pacing your climb, because each hairpin turn flattens the climb which you can use to your advantage, either taking each section for a respite, or speed up for a slingshot effect into the next corner.

Dutch Mountain is just one of the nicknames Alpe d'Huez bares, and nowhere on the climb symbolises this better than bend 7 – or what is otherwise known as Dutch Corner. At every Tour, thousands of Dutch fans gather here, often turning it into a week-long party with Europop blaring out into the night outside the quaint setting of the Saint Ferréol church that sits on the inside bend. The Dutch have had significant success on the climb with eight of the first 14 winners on the climb coming from the lowland nation.

The sight of the ski chalets high above

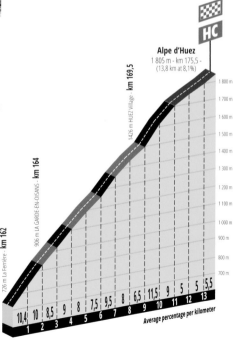

Alpe d'Huez
1 805 m - km 175,5 -
(13,8 km at 8,1%)

**KEY**

From 3 to 5,9 %

From 6 to 8,9 %

From 9 %

*Average percentage per kilometer*

as you reach the village of Huez will be a boost for your mind that the top isn't far away, and if you need one last drink or food stop, this will be your final chance before pushing on to the summit. It is also where the gradient kicks up once more and the hairpins become less frequent for the final few bends towards the town. Make sure you have your best power-pose on as a collection of photographers are stationed on these final few bends every day of the year to capture cyclists making the pilgrimage to "The Alp".

As you reach the town of Alpe d'Huez you may be tempted to stop amongst the shops and cafes with a number of finish lines signifying the top of the ascent. However, the Tour de France actually finishes a further kilometre above the town and if you've made it this far you'll feel guilty if you don't make it all the way to where the pros finish. The lack of shops or cafes may make it seem a little bit of an anti-climax on the Tour de France finishing straight, but it does have a podium for a picture-perfect moment before you descend back down to the town for a well-deserved rest and absorb the fact you have added your name to the long list of cyclists to have crested one of the sport's most iconic ascents.

▼ Each switchback on Alpe d'Huez is named after a previous winner of the stage the Alpe has hosted.

LENGTH: **20.8KM**
AVERAGE GRADIENT: **7.5%**
HEIGHT OF SUMMIT: **1,912M**
TOTAL METRES ASCENDED: **1,598M**

**The "Giant of Provence", "Bald Mountain" and "Beast of Provence" are just a few nicknames assigned to Mont Ventoux. Even though its standalone nature in the Provence region means that some do not consider it part of the Alps, it does, geologically-speaking, cling to the Western periphery of the Alpine mountain range.**

There are three routes up to the summit of Ventoux, from the settlements of Sault, Malaucène and Bédoin – with the challenge of riding up all three routes to the top in one day gaining admission to the Club des Cinglés du Mont-Ventoux. The last of these three routes is the classic and has been used

in multiple editions of the Tour de France.

Due to its remote and unique location, the summit of Ventoux sticks out on the landscape and gives the unique and rare experience of being able to see the top of the climb from the bottom, which is both inspiring and intimidating in equal amounts. Whereas the first few kilometres are gentle as the gradient slowly ticks up, the sight of Ventoux in the distance is imposing as the summit – looking snow-capped – looms large.

As the view of the Ventoux meteorological station disappears from sight as you enter the wooded section of the climb, the gradient bites and tops out in double figures. Ventoux's show-stopping upper section almost takes the attention away from the earlier slopes in the climb, which are arguably some of the toughest the mountain has to offer – often ramping above 12% gradient. Like a lot of alpine climbs, the distance can skew the average gradient and in this forest section is where Ventoux bites.

The sight of Chalet Reynard as you exit the woods is one that all cyclists crave, not only because they may be after a much-needed respite but also because the gradient lessens from this point. It also signals a shift in landscape from dense woodland to the famous lunar landscape, with the exposed terrain often leaving riders at the peril of the wind.

This rocky environment is actually limestone, and the sheer openness of the upper section of this climb is subjected to

▲ Chris Froome rode to glory ahead of Nairo Quintana on Ventoux in the 2013 Tour.

**MONT VENTOUX**
1 912 m - km 184 - (15,7 km à 8,8%)

1 435 m Chalet Reynard - km 178

536 m Saint-Estève - km 168,5

1 900 m
1 800 m
1 700 m
1 600 m
1 500 m
1 400 m
1 300 m
1 200 m
1 100 m
1 000 m
900 m
800 m
700 m
600 m
500 m

Average percentage per kilometer

| 9,5 | 9 | 10 | 8,5 | 9,3 | 9,5 | 8,5 | 9 | 7,5 | 7,5 | 5,5 | 8 | 7,5 | 8,3 | 9,2 | 9,5 |
|---|---|---|---|---|---|---|---|---|---|---|---|---|---|---|---|
| 1 | 2 | 3 | 4 | 5 | 6 | 7 | 8 | 9 | 10 | 11 | 12 | 13 | 14 | 15 | |

**KEY**
From 3 to 5,9 %
From 6 to 8,9 %
From 9 %

◄ The lunar landscape of Ventoux is one of the most iconic sights in pro cycling that fans flock to every time the mountain is on the route.

winds once recorded at 321kph (200mph). It is unlikely this will be the case in the summer months, when the climb is open, but this cannot be underestimated. If the wind isn't blowing, the heat can also be just as effective in disrupting a rider's rhythm on a sweltering hot day with no canopy shelter to shade under. The elements caused the Tour organisers – citing worries for spectators and riders alike – to amend the race route in 2016. High winds forced the finish line of stage 12 to Chalet Reynard to be moved and it had disastrous repercussions for maillot jaune Chris Froome, who crashed into a motorbike which couldn't make it through the dense crowds.

As the gradient hovers around a slightly more manageable 8–9% – compared to the forest section of the climb, the most notable landmark on the final grind to the line is the memorial dedicated to British cyclist Tommy Simpson, who tragically died on Ventoux during the 1967 Tour de France.

The final few kilometres seem to be never-ending as the sight of the famous telegraph pole and lighthouse tower slowly come into view before disappearing as the road swings back in against the mountain road. The final right-hand bend is a proper kicker and, if you aren't prepared, it might see you weaving across the road as you try to maintain momentum to the Ventoux sign plastered with stickers from visitors from around the world.

Ventoux sums up just why cyclists push themselves up these mythical ascents. The challenge of reaching the summit of this one of a kind monster that looms over the barren landscape is something each rider who crests it won't ever forget.

# RIDING IN THE VOSGES

**The Vosges may not have the towering beasts of the Alps, or the lengthy ascents of the Pyrenees, but in recent times it has become a well-visited Tour de France mountain range. The use of Planche des Belles Filles has taken the limelight in recent years with Chris Froome, Vincenzo Nibali and Fabio Aru all winning stages at the summit of the climb. But there is much more to riding in the Vosges than just the Planche, all of which are excellent for cyclists looking to explore the area.**

▲ Eddy Merckx took victory atop the Col d'Alsace on his way to his first Maillot Jaune in 1969.

The Grand Ballon is the highest mountain in the Vosges, topping out at 1,353 metres and averaging a little more than 6% gradient over the 15.6-kilometre climb. This is one of the longest climbs in the mountain range and is notable for its white giant radar tower which sits at the top. First appearing in the Tour in 1969, it has made six further appearances –most recently in 2014, when Tony Martin was the first over the summit on the way to the finish in Mulhouse.

With no major towns or cities nearby, it means that the roads of the Vosges are quiet and ideal for an off-the-grid cycling holiday which ticks all the boxes.

Two other climbs in the region also borrow the "Ballon" name – which, in geographical terms, translates to "rounded summit" – the Ballon d'Alsace and Ballon de Servance. The latter follows the same run in to Planche des Belles Filles, through the towns of Plancher-Bas and Plancher-les-Mines, before forking left at the base of the now perennial Tour de France finishing climb along the D16. After the turn-off, the false flat through the towns disappears and ramps up more than 9% in sections for the final 12 kilometres of the ascent to the summit at 1,158 metres.

The Ballon d'Alsace is shorter, at a little more than 9.1 kilometres, but it has a far steadier 6.9% gradient to tackle, and an extensive early history in the Tour de France. It was as far back as in 1905 that the Col d'Alsace became the first mountain ever to be crossed in the Tour de France, and it was subsequently used in the next seven editions of the race. It has also been used as a stage summit finish four times, including in 1969 when Eddy Merckx was on his way to winning his first maillot jaune.

As the Vosges region is close to the German, Swiss and Luxembourg borders and accessible for other parts of Northern Europe. It gives cycling fans a chance to drive to the mountains rather than fly further south to the Alps or Pyrenees.

One final Tour climb amateurs can take in is the Col des Chevrères. This short, sharp ascent from its northern side averages 9.5% gradient over 3.5 kilometres is an excellent warm-up for the Planche des Belles Filles, which sits across the valley. It was tackled in this order in both the 2014 and 2019 Tours de France.

# VOSGES TRAVEL GUIDE

**HOW TO GET THERE:** Basel Mulhouse Freiberg is the closest airport to the Vosges which is roughly a 1½- hour drive away from the Vosges. Strasbourg is an alternative but doesn't have direct flights from mainline United Kingdom like Basel.

**LOCATION IN FRANCE:** North-west close to the German and Swiss borders

**CLIMATE:** Wet outside of summer months but thanks to its lower mountain summits snow is a far less problem than the Alps or Pyrenees, which means that most roads will be open year-round.

**NEARBY CITIES:** Mulhouse, Basel and Strasbourg

▼ The Vosges mountains are a hidden gem when it comes to places cyclists must visit.

## MATT WINSTON – TEAM SUNWEB COACH

"The Vosges is a little bit untapped. The Tour has not spent too much time in the region, or you arrive there and it heads straight up the climbs, but they are pretty steep in certain points. Even though the Alps and Pyrenees are the focal points and that is where everyone wants to go ride but actually it is also pretty hard riding in the Vosges. There are some pretty heavy roads, and they are quite draining. The roads between the climbs in the valleys are not the easiest to ride either, and it feels grippy all the time.

"You may not get the proper high mountains, but you do get a real good workout if you ride in that region. Planche des Belles Filles has become a bit of a focal point on the Tour and it's interesting to see them still experimenting with it, such as the gravel section and a time trial on the penultimate day of the race."

The Vosges mountains can offer just as challenging and picturesque climbs in their own right.

# CLIMBS OF THE TOUR
# PLANCHE DES BELLES FILLES
## APPROACH VIA PLANCHER-LES-MILNES

LENGTH: **7KM**
AVERAGE GRADIENT: **8.7%**
HEIGHT OF SUMMIT: **1,140M**
TOTAL METRES ASCENDED: **608M**

▲ Chris Froome broke free from Cadel Evans and Bradley Wiggins on the final steep ramp to win in 2012.

**Considering this climb was used for the first time in the 2012 Tour de France, it has quickly grown to become one of the modern icons of the race. It may not have the length or height of its Pyrenean or Alpine cousins, but it has played a defining role in each edition of the Tour in which it has featured. Tour organisers continue to come back and tweak its make-up to constantly keep the peloton on its toes.**

Just north of the village of Plancher-les-Mines, the road to Planche des Belles Filles turns off the D16 onto the D16E. There is a sign at the bottom signifying Chris Froome's record breaking ascent on Stage

7 in 2012 – it was also where fellow Briton Bradley Wiggins took the maillot jaune and kept it all the way to Paris. The placard also breaks down the climb into its average gradients for each section, but this may prove a tad intimidating for the ride ahead.

After turning off the D16, the road immediately heads skywards, with the imposing gradient hitting you with full force as it weaves its way up into the woods. The one psychological plus-point, when tackling the Planche, is the fact that it is shorter than any other iconic Tour climb. This may feel like little respite as you struggle to tap out a rhythm as ramps of 13% stunt your progress, then drop momentarily before kick up once more.

Unlike other climbs, the five hairpin corners that are dotted on the way up to the original Tour summit allow for little respite, maintaining their harsh gradient through the bend and onto the next straight. This isn't to say the gradient is consistent all the way up, which makes it crucial you are on top of your gearing at all times and don't get caught out. This is especially so in a devious lull before a devilish steep kick to the line which may see professionals blast their way up, but mere mortals will be weaving to maintain traction and speed. It isn't surprising as at 20%, finding traction on a damp day may be even more of a worry than usual.

Upon reaching the top of this almighty ramp – which only consists of a couple of hundred metres but feels like an eternity – feel free to take a minute a compare your

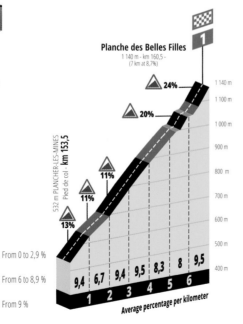

**Planche des Belles Filles**
1 140 m - km 160,5 - (7 km at 8,7%)

532 m PLANCHER-LES-MINES
Pied de col - **km 153,5**

24% — 1 140 m
1 100 m
20% — 1 000 m
900 m
11% 800 m
11% 700 m
13% 600 m
500 m
400 m

**KEY**

From 0 to 2,9 %
From 6 to 8,9 %
From 9 %

| 9,4 | 6,7 | 9,4 | 9,5 | 8,3 | 8 | 9,5 |
|---|---|---|---|---|---|---|
| 1 | 2 | 3 | 4 | 5 | 6 | |

*Average percentage per kilometer*

times at the classic Tour de France finish line to those marked on the road and see where Froome, Vincenzo Nibali and Fabio Aru have all taken stage glory.

If you want an added challenge, there is a sting in this Vosges demon's tail because, in 2019, race organisers added a twist to the already-savage ascent. They added a further kilometre to what can only be described as a wood-lined strip of gravel track, that rises through the trees to an ungodly wall-like section that touches 24% gradient in its final stretches. It is not a case of riding this section fast, but there is the challenge of sustaining your cadence and

not to put you foot down.

Once you regain your breath at this new finish line, the reward on a clear day from this true summit of the climb are worth the ride, with breathtaking views back towards Champagney and beyond.

With the Tour de France returning to Planche des Belles Filles in 2020, this time on the penultimate stage of the entire race, the rider wearing yellow after a gruelling individual time trial will be locked in to finish top of the General Classification. It seems certain that more dramatic Tour history will continue to be made and the legacy of this secluded summit will continue to grow.

▼ The addition of a gravel stretch of road at the summit was an intriguing twist from race organisers in 2019.

Escaping the winter months for sunnier climates can be the perfect way to augment your training.

TOUR de France

CHAPTER 16

# TRAINING CAMPS

A training camp can be a great way of getting a set training block under your belt in a cycling paradise. Different locations have different benefits, whether it is preparing for the high mountains of a Grand Tour or just focusing for a concentrated period with team-mates. Training camps can be a perfect physical and – perhaps more important – psychological boost to your training programme.

# MAKING TRAINING CAMPS WORK FOR YOU

▲ Having a focused block of training away from the distractions of home can be really beneficial.

**If you are looking to mix up your training in the lead up to your event later in the year, training camps are an excellent way of achieving this. They not only provide a consistent block of training without the distractions of work or other commitments but also typically provide better weather and roads than are found around your local area.**

There are a few key points you should research, depending on your individual needs. The first of these should be when – and to where – you plan to fly out. Heading out in the summer months usually

guarantees good weather in most cycling destinations, however, spring or autumn can prove trickier if you are heading to high altitude, where it may still be subject to the elements with boiling hot weather one day followed by rain or even snow the next. Even though you'll be keen to smash your way on training rides in dreamy cycling locations. It is important not to overdo it as you could make yourself ill or injured immediately after your camp and find yourself out of action and back to where you started pre-trip.

It is also important not to get too competitive with whoever you are on your holiday, it may be tempting to duel it out with certain riding mates, and there

## TUSCANY TRAVEL GUIDE

**AIRPORTS:** Pisa, Florence

**BEST TIME OF YEAR TO VISIT:** March, April, May

**PROS:** Lots of quiet roads and varied terrain; beautiful surroundings; good food

**CONS:** Heavy traffic in busier areas; no big climbs; few cycling-focused hotels

**FAMOUS FOR:** Iconic white roads; glorious scenery

▶ It may not have the high mountain passes of Alps or Pyrenees but there are some wonderful climbs to conquer.

## CÔTE D'AZUR TRAVEL GUIDE

**AIRPORTS:** Nice

**BEST TIME OF YEAR TO VISIT:** March, April, May

**PROS:** Huge variety of routes and reliable weather

**CONS:** Busy roads around the coast

**FAMOUS FOR:** Col de Madone, Col d'Eze, Col de Turini

▲ Arguably the most picturesque location to ride a bike, Tuscany is perfect both on and off bike for a training camp.

is certainly a time to do it with the odd sprint for the sign post. However, getting involved in a battle royal up a 30-kilometre mountain climb may not be ideal. Training camps are about improving yourself, rather than proving yourself to others. France, Spain and Italy are just some of the travel choices of the pros, but there are plenty of destinations making their mark and becoming available to cyclists every year.

### WHY TRAINING CAMPS ARE CRUCIAL FOR THE PROS: NICO PORTAL, TEAM INEOS DIRECTEUR SPORTIF

When you start to race, you race for a team you cannot race for yourself. Other sports know the season is coming, so they can adjust their team and, within a couple of weeks, they know they'll play in the same stadium, train together every day and talk about things like tactics or any other issues.

In cycling, however, we are always moving and in different locations, either in the UK, France, Spain and we could be up a mountain where the connection isn't great. For example, in 2019, I saw Michal Golas for one day in Majorca and then nothing at all for the rest of the season.

It's the same with staff members, as we may not do the same race. There are so many races we may have three teams racing in three different countries at the same time. The first training camp we have is more of a team camp where all the riders, wherever they live, have to come to Majorca. We sit together, have a briefing, train together, and it is the first time we talk to new colleagues, mechanics and team mates and start our team building, which is really important. They have a good ten-day block of training to start them off, with good food, good massages and we make sure their first block of endurance is perfect.

# TRAINING CAMPS

# MAJORCA AND CALPE

▲ Chris Froome won atop the Cumbre del Sol just outside of Calpe in the 2017 Vuelta a Espana.

Head to Majorca, or the south-east coast of Spain, in December and January and you shouldn't be surprised to see bundles of UCI WorldTour and ProTeams setting up for team camps for the winter months. In what is the off-season for most of these summer coastal resorts, the pilgrimage of hundreds of cyclists has been a massive boost for their economy and has helped improve the cycling infrastructure in both regions.

In Majorca, there are a couple of must-ride climbs and sights to take in, and one of the most ascended climbs every year is Sa Calobra, or the Coll dels Reis, as it is also known. It will probably never feature in a race due to it being a dead-end road, but it is unique to pros and amateurs as the ultimate climb first has to be descended to the coast, then ridden back up to the summit. At just under ten kilometres, and averaging 7%, it isn't too taxing for most strong cyclists, and the only issue for most will be the stunning scenery back down towards the base of the climb that can take your breath away. Some of the highlights include: the famous rock arch where two rocks have collapsed on each other creating a perfect road sized gap in between and the ever-changing road direction that mimics a shoelace draped on a mountain. However, the best is saved until last: a show-stopping 270-degree final corner that corkscrews back on itself; it is the perfect way to end a picture-perfect climb.

## MAJORCA TRAVEL GUIDE

**AIRPORTS:** Palma

**BEST TIME OF YEAR TO VISIT:** January, March, April, May

**PROS:** Variety of terrain, quiet roads, cycling-friendly hotels, good climbs, lots of riders

**CONS:** Weather can be unreliable in winter months

**FAMOUS FOR:** Sa Calobra and Puig Major.

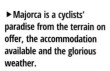

▶ Majorca is a cyclists' paradise from the terrain on offer, the accommodation available and the glorious weather.

Be careful of the stunning scenery as it is not only cyclists who converge on the climb, but also tourist buses and cars make their way to this beauty spot during the peak hours of the day. Therefore, it is best to ride up it in the early morning or late afternoon.

Other climbs, such as Puig Major and the Coll de Sóller, also offer the opportunity for cyclists to explore different parts of the island. Also, some of the most hardy cyclists go so far as to test their bodies over an entire lap of the island.

Another Spanish getaway for cyclists is the Costa Blanca coastline on the Mediterranean coast, which is Calpe, the site of the perennial training camp for the pros. The attraction of Calpe in the early months of the year is the local weather. With more than 320 days of sunshine a year, it is rare that you won't be treated to some winter doses of vitamin D.

The riding for cyclists is also varied for all abilities, with steady climbs of 6%, including the Coll de Rates, which holds a manageable 5% to the summit. It features old-school timing ticket machines at the base and summit of the climb to time your ascent. There is terrain of the short and steep variety, that have been used in previous editions of the Vuelta a España, notably the Cumbre del Sol, which featured as summit-finishes in both the 2015 and 2017 editions. It may only be a touch over four kilometres in length, but it reaches more than double-digit figures in gradient. Once you reach the summit, the vast landscape and views down the coast towards Calpe and the razor-tooth-like rock Penyal d'Ifac, which sticks out from the coast are worth the ascent.

▼ Calpe and the surrounding region is a hotbed for professional teams during pre season.

## CALPE TRAVEL GUIDE

**AIRPORTS:** Alicante

**BEST TIME OF YEAR TO VISIT:** January, February, March

**PROS:** Reliable weather, affordable hotels.

**CONS:** Few big climbs, heavy traffic in places.

**FAMOUS FOR:** Coll de Rates and Cumbre del Sol.

# GIRONA AND THE HOME OF THE PROS

▲ The medieval city is a must visit if you are looking for great cycling camp both on and off the bike.

**There are a number of hubs across the world which attract cyclists to set up their seasons, whether it be Andorra for the pro peloton's mountain goats or the French Riviera of Monaco and Nice for others. In recent times, however, Girona has become the training camp home or base of the pro rider. Many of the best cyclists are often seen in the coffee shops of the Catalonian town – as well as racking up miles on the local roads.**

The medieval city itself, on first observation, may not be seen as a cyclist's hub with its cobbled streets and mazy roads weaving their way in, around and out of the town. But the country lanes surrounding the walled town are a pro cyclist's paradise. With the headline climb of Girona being the now infamous Rocacorba, which is often used as a testing ground for pro riders to see where their form is prior to a big race.

Situated about 20 kilometres north of Girona, the climb is just over 13 kilometres, rising 881 metres at an average of 6.5%. This average gradient is teasing, but it does include a number of

▶ The varied terrain makes it perfect for cyclists of all abilities.

## GIRONA TRAVEL GUIDE

**AIRPORTS:** Barcelona and Girona

**BEST TIME OF YEAR TO VISIT:** March, April or May

**PROS:** Quiet roads and a nice town to visit

**CONS:** Only a few big climbs within easy riding distance

**FAMOUS FOR:** Rocacorba

▲ The summit of Rocacorba has become a niche cycling mecca of recent times.

kilometres into double-digits, with pitches in gradient that max out at 15%. The road was only fully paved in 2006, but it is the highest climb in the area, with its peak of 991 metres dwarfing the hills around it.

The climb starts off pretty gently for the first few kilometres out of Banyoles but it gives you a preview into just how varied the gradient is on Rocacorba. This makes it hard to find a rhythm all the way up to the summit, and the pace disruption will be stunted as a brutish 12% section hits around half way up the climb. It eases briefly into a short descent after four kilometres, before a final steep section to the top. Rocacorba is one of those climbs which is a dead-end road, enjoyed solely by cyclists who want to suffer to the summit and test their bodies to the limit. For a pro, the gold marker time is anything under 30 minutes, whereas for amateurs just taking in the views at the summit can be the reward for a solid riding effort.

Cycling infrastructure in Girona doesn't only consist of the roads, terrain and traffic; the life of a pro cyclist often means regularly jumping on planes to a race, or heading to other team training camp locations. Therefore, the ease of having both Girona and Barcelona airports relatively on your doorstep is an attractive proposition for pros who live there, as well as for the cycling tourists who want to visit the region.

### PRO INSIGHT: MITCHELL DOCKER, RIDER, EF PRO CYCLING

I currently live up in Andorra, but I've been based between Andorra and Girona for the last eight years. It has got a lot to do with the training, because training there is pretty good and you can do everything. You can go to the mountains, as well as to the coast, and the traffic is great.

# TENERIFE, TEIDE AND ALTITUDE

**The Canary Islands, just off the north-west coast of Africa, has gained a reputation over recent times as the must-visit destination for not only holiday-makers seeking year-round sun, but also cyclists looking for altitude-training and reliable weather.**

Mount Teide – which is actually an active volcano – sits in the middle of the island and, at 2,200 metres, the discreet-looking Hotel Parador, which sits within the volcano crater, is a magnet for professional cyclists looking for year-round altitude-training in preparation for the Grand Tours.

What is also unique about Teide is that you can start your ascent from the town of Los Cristianos at sea level on the coast. Reaching the summit is equal to 33 kilometres of continuous ascent. There are alternative routes up to the summit, but

this is arguably the most picturesque – once you start to climb away from the busier coastal towns. This lengthy ascent changes continuously all the way to the summit, from busy tourist towns, constant switchbacks on the open lower slopes, to a wooded section above the clouds and into the barren landscape of the volcano crater at the top.

The gradient is pretty steady all the way up to the summit through the ever-changing sections of road. It is more the length of the climb and total elevation which will drain cyclists physiologically, most of all once the climb rises above 1,500 metres, when the significant altitude effects come into play.

The effect of altitude is down to the reduction of oxygen particles in the air. At sea level, your oxygen saturation level (SpO2) will be around 95 to 100, where oxygen content within the air is 21 per cent. Once you rise above 2,000 metres,

▲ The Hotel Parador is a haven for pro cyclists to escape to altitude in the lead up to Grand Tours.

▶ Being able to ride from sea level to over 2,000 metres makes Mount Teide one of the most unique climbs in the world.

## TENERIFE TRAVEL GUIDE

**AIRPORTS:** Palma

**CLIMATE:** Sunny year round

**PROS:** Altitude training on Mount Teide

**CONS:** Limited routes other than climbing

**FAMOUS FOR:** Mount Teide

▲ **Mount Teide is still an active volcano but is the ultimate for all round altitude training.**

the oxygen in the air drops to 15 per cent, which has a knock-on consequence on SpO2 levels to drop to around 80. This makes exercise not only feel harder but also gives the body a stimulus to adapt to.

This is why professional cyclists train at altitude to replicate the conditions they will experience during the Tour de France. The secluded Hotel Parador is regularly booked-up by professional teams before Grand Tours so their riders can sleep at altitude and then drop down to a more manageable altitude to train and retain the physiological benefits.

### NICO PORTAL – TEAM INEOS SPORTS DIRECTOR

Altitude training is really important. We have specific training camps for the Grand Tours, where the riders will head to altitude for 10 days to two weeks. The guys who live

at altitude stay there, but for a GC racer it is super-important to train at altitude for a couple of weeks to reach the next level. On Teide, you put yourself into a bubble and there is not much of a distraction, there is only one hotel up there, no shops or anything else. It is like a moon on the top so you are just thinking about the Tour and you get mentally stronger for it by avoiding any distractions. The last few days can be quite hard mentally as well as physically, but when they finish training camp they know they are really ready to go.

In the 2019 Tour we knew that the last week was pretty hard, we had done the recon for stage 19, and knew from halfway onwards you would reach 1,600 metres and stay there for the second half of the stage. If you don't pace yourself for two hours above that elevation then you can lose everything, so training at altitude is crucial to winning the Tour de France.

The training and preparation is done, now it is time to conquer the Étape du Tour

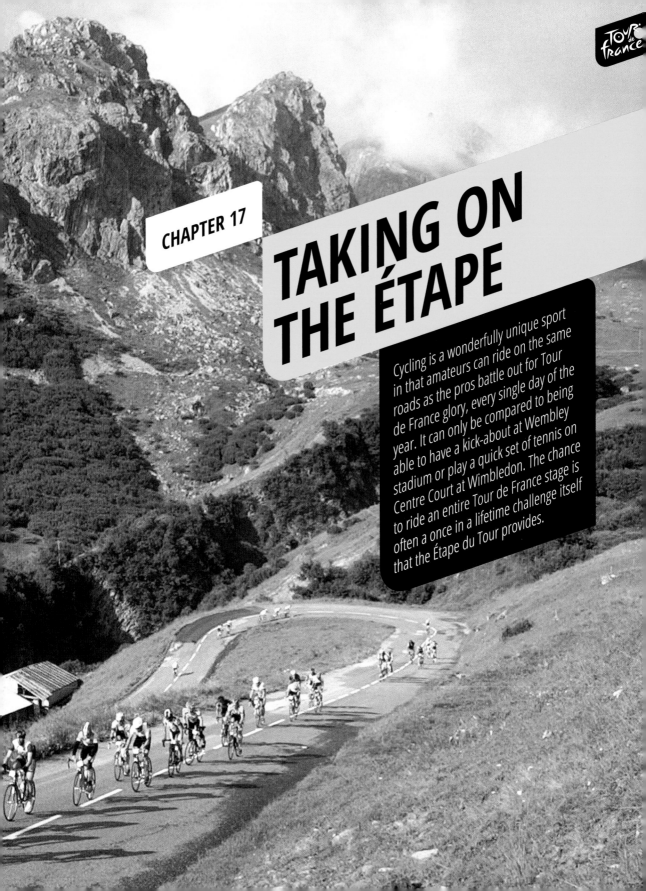

CHAPTER 17

# TAKING ON THE ÉTAPE

Cycling is a wonderfully unique sport in that amateurs can ride on the same roads as the pros battle out for Tour de France glory, every single day of the year. It can only be compared to being able to have a kick-about at Wembley stadium or play a quick set of tennis on Centre Court at Wimbledon. The chance to ride an entire Tour de France stage is often a once in a lifetime challenge itself that the Étape du Tour provides.

# PREPARING FOR THE L'ÉTAPE DU TOUR

**One of the biggest and most gruelling single-day amateur sportive events on the cycling calendar is the L'Étape du Tour. Replicating a stage of that year's Tour de France is sometimes a once in a lifetime chance for cyclists to tackle what the professionals face over three intensive weeks of racing. Despite the months of training required to ride and complete these events, it is crucial to ensure you prepare in the correct way in the week leading up to the big day.**

▼ Heading out for a pre ride spin the day before the event is an ideal way to shake out your travel legs.

One important thing for cyclists to take on board is that their bike set-up at home may not be suited for long days in the saddle. There is nothing macho about riding around with huge gears that once you reach the second climb of the day you can't even turn around. Therefore, fitting a compact groupset (50–34) on the front and a larger chainring on the back for emergencies is always a useful tactic.

The training required to take on these long-distance rides is evident to all who enter them and long, sustained training rides of six hours are considered the minimum recommendation. However, once you arrive at your destination, ensuring you loosen your legs – just as after a flight or long car journey – should be considered a top priority. This isn't a case of recce-ing one of the climbs and burning precious energy before the big day; going for a short ride to loosen the legs the day before is the perfect prescription for success. A steady, hour-long ride with a couple of efforts to blow away any cobwebs and stimulate any lactate clearance is ideal preparation. Heading out for a ride also helps the body acclimatise to altitude, which will be more than likely be the case for the Étape.

Many people make the mistake of trying something new on event day, or in the hours leading up to an event. Even if you are in a foreign country, you should be aware of what nutritional meals work for you and what don't. Sticking to the same meal plans you would have at home the night before will result in no

## FIVE TOP TIPS TO NAIL THE ÉTAPE

- Take an old jumper or jacket to wear to the start. If you have to descend down a mountain in the early hours, it is highly likely to be cold.

- Try and learn a few useful foreign phrases that could help you out if in mechanical and nutritional need.

- Prepare your bike and lay out clothing the day before, giving you peace of mind knowing that everything is ready to go in the morning.

- Pace yourself for the ride ahead. Climbing multiple mountains is different to a hill-repeat session back home. Ensuring you still have enough left in the tank for the finish push will be crucial.

- Don't rely on airlines to automatically accept your bicycle as standard hold luggage. Check before you travel so you don't have to pay extra at the airport.

▼ Laying out your kit the day before will ensure you don't forget anything on the big day itself.

nasty surprises. It is also the same when preparing your on-bike nutrition the night before, as a number of riders fail to prepare for the change in nutritional demands that is placed on the body. This could be demanding temperatures that require a strict nutrition protocol, which in turn replicate an eating and drinking contest on the bike if riding for multiple hours.

Riding with friends in moderate climate conditions is one thing, but this lack of attention to nutrition can rack up over time and you'll pay the price for poor nutrition in these longer events. Aiming to get 500ml of fluid and 60g of carbohydrate per hour is a good starting point to aim for, and adjust accordingly depending your personal needs. Eating little and often is smarter than large consumption spaced out over longer distances.

▲ Hitting the wall or bonking can be avoided by eating and drinking throughout your ride.

You may be half asleep, wide awake or in a deep snooze, but the beep of the alarm clock will more than likely jolt you out of sleep on the morning of the Étape. No matter how well you slept, today is the day and, the chances are, you will be an early riser in preparation for your start time. Getting a solid and hearty breakfast may be difficult, but you'll be grateful as soon as you are on the bike.

When you are waiting in your start pen, take in the moment and don't be afraid. Pre-ride nerves are a good thing; embrace them knowing that you are getting ready to ride something for which you are prepared. Even if you think you are the least prepared person around you, don't worry. It is almost impossible to find a cyclist who has prepared immaculately in the build-up to the big day.

When the gun goes, take it easy. The adrenaline will be pumping and as you will be feeling fresh, you'll want to shoot out to a lightning-fast start, but it is crucial to think of the bigger picture. In your mind give yourself psychological checkpoints to tick off along the way.

This makes the challenge of a long day in the saddle much easier when chunked up into manageable sections.

The first climb on any Granfondo is always going to be chaotic to say the least; riders want to show their strength and smash it up the first climb. Whereas some of these riders may be genuine mountain goats, a large chunk will be burning too many matches too soon. Others will look in a world of pain for whatever reason.

Hopefully you'll be able to pace your own ride, taking in checkpoints that you've highlighted before the ride and making steady progress to the summit.

It is important to remember to eat

## THREE TIPS TO HAVING A GREAT ÉTAPE

- Pacing – Don't worry about anyone else, stick to your strategy and don't get forced into riding a faster pace if it isn't in your comfort zone.

- Eat and drink your way to the finish – Staying fuelled and hydrated is vital on a long ride. Don't skip that feed station if you are running with empty bottles; the five minutes lost filling them up will be doubled if you suffer on your way to the summit.

- Celebrate your achievement – You have prepared for this for months. Don't underestimate just how proud you should be and be sure to treat yourself to an alcoholic beverage or cheat meal afterwards. You've earned it!

and drink as little and often as you can. You should have a decent idea from your training just how much you need to consume and when, but a long day in the saddle with the excitement of thousands of other riders can distract you and may give you an unintentional lift before the inevitable bonk arrives.

The final climb always shows who has trained — and perhaps more importantly who has paced their effort to perfection. There will be riders slowing to a standstill, or walking their bike up a climb with the noise of their cleats slapping against the road. If you are starting to flag, focusing on a mark further up the road will help eliminate the overall challenge in front of you.

Then comes the thrill of the finish, and it is one you should definitely soak up, this ride is something you have worked hard for months to achieve and it is no mean feat. The high of conquering the climbs of that day will be euphoric, perhaps enough to immediately start planning for next year …

▼ Pacing your ride is crucial to ensuring you aren't flagging on the final climb.

Combining your Étape experience with a visit to the Tour itself is the perfect way to appreciate the skill of the pros.

# GET OUT THERE AND RIDE

▲ The journey when training for a Gran Fondo is just as challenging as the ride itself.

▶ The open road is out there to be explored. So go hit it!

**The training and/or nutrition advice given throughout this book will be of great benefit to your riding, and I hope you have taken it. This may culminate in you taking your first steps into the world of cycling, improving your efficiency on the bike or even helping you on your way to completing the Étape du Tour itself.**

But, most importantly, I hope that it inspires you to just go out there and ride, whether it is riding along your local lanes, venturing further afield and exploring the mammoth mountains ranges of mainland Europe or even the challenges offered on other continents.

One of the joys of cycling is that every ride is different. They all have their own stories to tell, whether they are from the sights you see on the way, the personal bests you achieve in races or challenges, or simply the friendships you make within the sport.

What is also fantastic about the current state of cycling is that there is an ever-changing landscape off the bike too, in training, nutrition and technology. The implementation of team chefs are a recent phenomenon and power-meters are now commonplace amongst amateurs, A little more than 20 years ago, they were cutting-edge technology, available only for a minority of professional cyclists.

These tools that trickle down to the amateur ranks allow for a comparison and appreciation for how hard professional cyclists train to reach the pinnacle of the sport. The three weeks of gruelling racing over 21 stages test to their limit every one of the 176 riders who line up at the start. They will encounter wind, changing conditions, the heat and altitude of the high mountains and chilly downpours on cobbled roads.

With stage wins often coming down to millimetre differences, the importance of a strong team is just as crucial out on the road as well as behind the scenes. They help support the riders all the way to the top in the biggest races each and every season.

There is no greater testing ground, location and thrill for an amateur ride to compare themselves with the icons of cycling than on the grandest climbs of them all in France. This is where the greats of the sport have made their mark throughout the history of the Tour de France. The race and the mountains work together to create mythical ascents and a number of these have been featured earlier in the book. If you have the opportunity to visit them, either for training purposes, riding a Grand Fondo or viewing the Tour live in person, then grab it with both hands.

Some of the hidden goat tracks and quiet roads also provide stunning vistas to reward your hard riding, but the most important thing of all to remember is that no matter where you are in the world, you are riding actually out there riding.

As the great Eddy Merckx once said: "Ride as much or as little, as long or as short as you feel. But ride."

# INDEX

▶ Conquering the climbs of the Tour de France is a never ending journey of exploration and enjoyment.

The publishers would like to thank the following sources for their kind permission to reproduce the pictures in this book. Key: T=top, B=bottom, L=left, R=right.

**ASO:** /Pauline Ballet: 174; /Alex Broadway: 200-201
**GETTY IMAGES:** /Duncan Andison: 22BR; /Luk Benies/AFP: 186BR; /Marco Bertorello/AFP: 117, 167; /Lionel Bonaventure/AFP: 120BR, 155; /Luc Claessen: 13, 18-19B, 19T, 23, 26TL, 33, 71, 90BR, 103, 106BR, 108-109, 110TL; /Jean-Pierre Clatot/AFP: 173; /Philippe Cohat: 156-157; /Tim de Waele: 6, 7,10-11, 12TL, 15, 18TL, 28-29, 37, 42BR, 48BR, 55, 66TL, 72, 73, 75, 77, 83, 84, 86-87, 92BR, 94BR, 97, 102TL, 102BL, 107, 110BR, 112TL, 112BR, 121, 152-153, 160, 161, 164, 165, 170, 186TL, 188TL; /EyesWideOpen: 192TL, 192BR; /Andre Ferreira/Icon Sport: 24TL; /Franck Fife/AFP: 78-79; /Chris Graythen: 30-31, 63TR, 94TL, 111, 123; /Pascal Guyot/AFP: 98TL; /Humonia: 24BR; /Bryn Lennon: 38BR, 68-69, 85, 89, 176, 179; /Jeff Pachoud/AFP: 61, 106TL, 147, 166BL; /Justin Paget: 8-9, 20-21, 25, 58-59, 98-99, 100-101, 118-119, 124, 126-127, 129, 130, 133, 135, 140, 144-145, 146, 148, 149, 150-151, 196, 197, 202, 203, 207; /Christophe Pallot/Agence Zoom: 168-169; /Pascal Pavani/AFP: 50-51; /Doug Pensinger: 47, 62; /Piola666: 80TL; /Pixdeluxe: 125, 143; /Pascal Pochard Casabianca/AFP: 60BR; /Primeimages: 26BR; /Robertus Pudyanto: 34TL; /Lars Ronberg/FrontzoneSport: 96; /Joel Saget/AFP: 45; /Justin Setterfield: 52BR, 57, 189; /Peter Thompson/Heritage Images: 193; /Thomas Tolstrup: 139; /torwai: 116; /Kenzo Tribouillard/AFP: 34BR, 44; /Kei Tsuji: 39, 114, 115, 171; /Jean-Christophe Verhaegen/AFP: 180-181; /Wsfurlan: 80BR
**OFFSIDE SPORTS PHOTOGRAPHY:** /L'Equipe: 64, 66BR, 150TL, 154TL, 154BL, 158, 159T, 162, 163, 166TL, 175, 177, 178, 182, 194-195, 198, 199; /Presse Sports: 40-41, 60TL, 65, 159BR, 172, 183
**SHUTTERSTOCK:** /Adriaticfoto: 105;/U.J. Alexander: 22TL; /Antb: 54; /Juanan Barros Moreno: 90TL; /Bonn A: 52TL; /BublikHaus: 35; /Corepics VOF: 36; /Josep Curto: 191; /Digoarpi: 190TL; /Dolomite-summits: 136; /Oleg Elkov: 88; /Encierro: 184-185; /Bogdan Ionescu: 46; /Katiaishere: 190BR; /Kovop58: 16, 188BR; /Jacob Lund: 14, 42TL; /Chz Mhong: 17; /Microgen: 137; /Oleksandra Naumenko: 92TL; /Photoschmidt: 28TL; /Nikolas profoto: 187; /Sportpoint: 104; /Josep Suria: 12BR; /Torwaistudio: 32; /Simon Wilkinson/SWPix.com: 56TL, 56BR; /Wk1003mike: 38TL
**SWPix.com:** /Simon Wilkinson: 48TL, 74
**YAZURU SUNADA:** 120TL
**TEAM SUNWEB:** 76; /Vincent Riemersma: 70
**WELBECK PUBLISHING:** /Andy Jones: 63BL, 82

Every effort has been made to acknowledge correctly and contact the source and/or copyright holder of each picture any unintentional errors or omissions will be corrected in future editions of this book.